DRAWING
PERSPECTIVE

by Yves **Leblanc**

rockynook

I want to thank all of my students who, thanks to their pertinent questions and attentive listening, allowed me to delve into the delightful problem of representation. Many of these students of mine are now themselves teaching art and design in turn, and I take great pride in that.

DRAWING: Perspective

Yves Leblanc

Editor: Jocelyn Howell

Project manager: Lisa Brazieal

Marketing manager: Koryn Olage

Layout and type: Anthony Paular Design

Front cover and interior design: Sophie Charbonnel

Cover production: Anthony Paular Design

Cover illustrations: Yves Leblanc

Translation: Marie Deer

ISBN: 979-8-88814-365-0

(1st printing, April 2025)

© 2025 Yves Leblanc

Rocky Nook Inc.

1010 B Street, Suite 350

San Rafael, CA 94901

USA

Original French title: *La perspective par Yves Leblanc*

© 2024, Éditions Eyrolles, Paris, France

Distributed in the UK and Europe by Publishers Group UK

Distributed in the U.S. and all other territories by Publishers Group West

This book is printed on acid-free paper.

Printed in China

CONTENTS

Basic Concepts **4**

Introduction 4

The Horizon 6

Vanishing Points 8

Perceived Space 10

Construction Strategies **12**

Right Angles 12

Slopes 14

Triangulation 16

Measurements 18

Distances 20

Enhancements **22**

Ellipses 22

Shadows 24

Reflections 26

Digging Deeper **28**

3D Perspective 28

Panoramas 30

Resources 32

Introduction

Drawing, Seeing, and Translating

Our eyes see; our brain perceives. Perspective lies at the intersection of vision and perception.

Behind our eyes, our brain tries to establish a connection between the hemispheric projection of the retina and the space experienced by our body. That space is a three-dimensional space made up of heights, widths, and depths. The artist tries to translate all of these into their drawing.

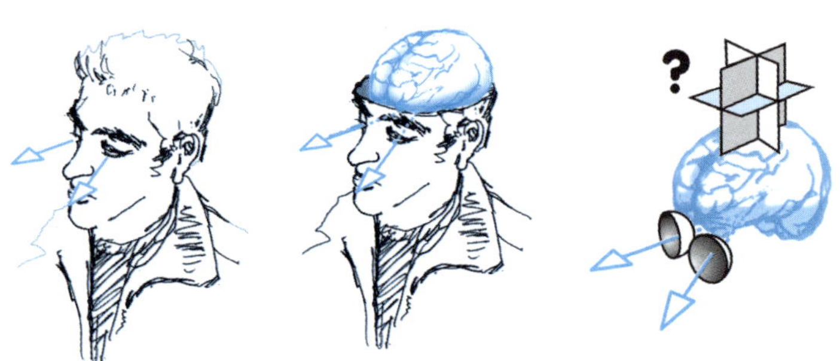

Drawing a Space

This is a matter of transferring onto a page what we could trace on an imaginary window placed between us and what we are looking at.

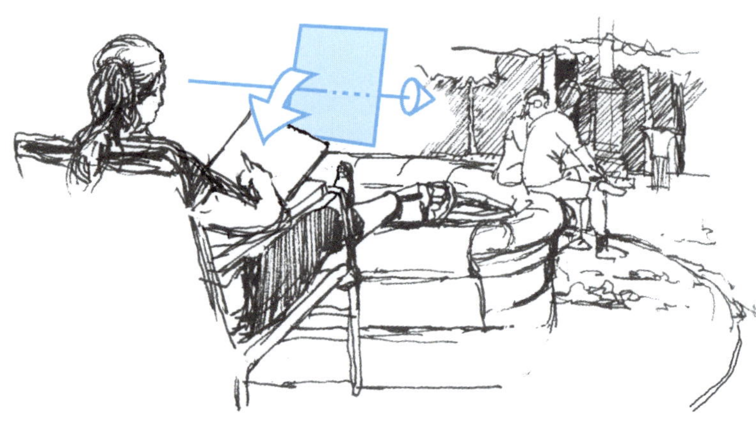

Paris, Garden of the Palais-Royal

Progression

The first three concepts covered in this book (the visual field, the horizon, and the vanishing point) can be considered in any order and do not have a hierarchical relationship among them.

The visual field, which we look at in the introduction, refers to our consciousness of the area viewed and the space to be transcribed.

The horizon relates to the space in which we are immersed and the location of our eyes.

The vanishing point refers to the direction of the objects in our environment in relation to the direction of our gaze.

Once we have absorbed these concepts, we will be able to juggle among them to establish analyses that allow us to reproduce **perceived space**.

Then we will be able to point out directions, define **right angles,** and calculate **slopes**.

Triangulation will allow us to obtain precise **measurements** and establish consistent **distances**.

Then, we will look at some enhancements—such as **omissions**, **shadows**, and **reflections**—in order to make our drawings more believable.

Finally, we will briefly invoke the principle of non-horizontal vision with **3D perspective** and the possibilities of drawing an enlarged visual field thanks to **panoramic views.**

Conical Perspective

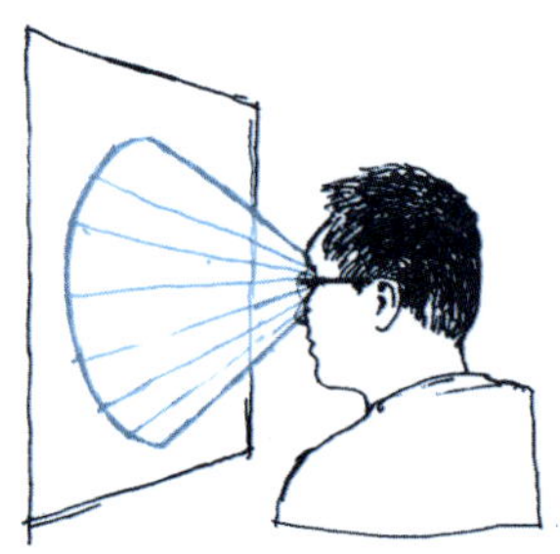

The perspective that we will be studying at first is called "**conical perspective**," because it is the projection of a space according to a cone of projection.

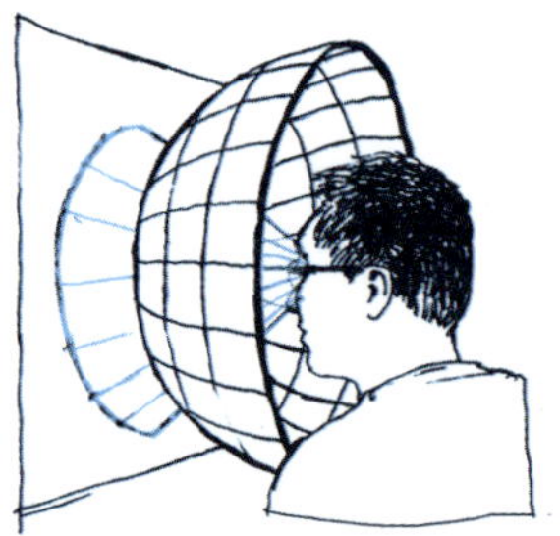

This only makes up part of the **hemispheric** perception of our environment.

The Visual Field

Our visual field constitutes about 180°, but only 120° of those degrees are simultaneously visible with both eyes (60° on each side). Beyond that, even though we are aware of the space around us, it is impossible to translate it without it being distorted.

In order to understand our binocular visual field, we have to identify the limits of our left-right vision with the opposing eye; this gives us a global angle of 120°.

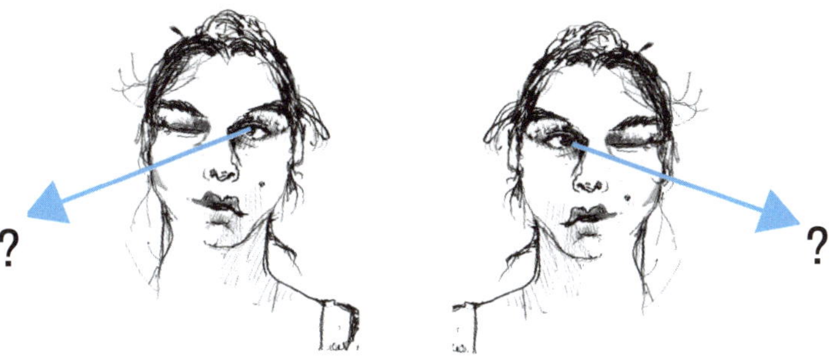

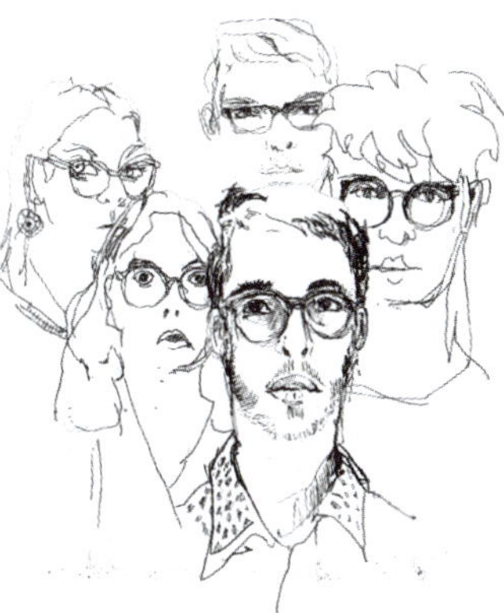

Our visual field can be understood more clearly with glasses, as their edges provide additional markers.

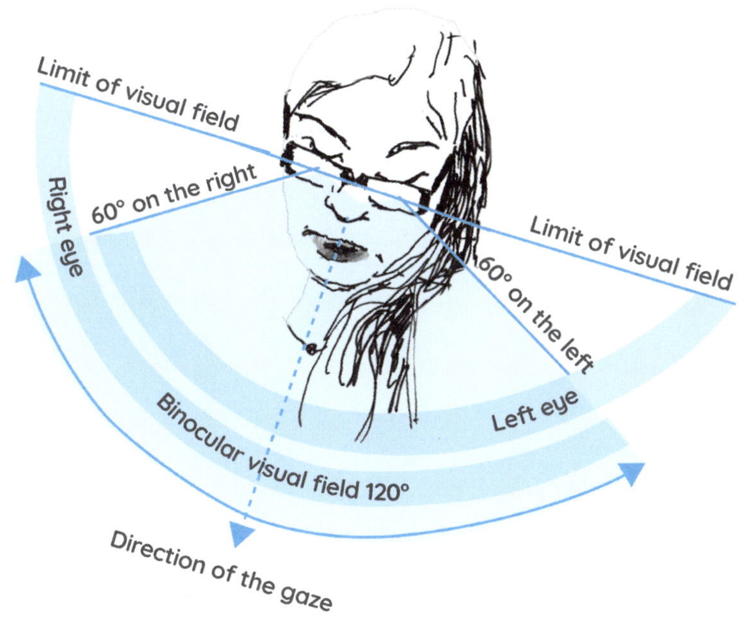

Distortions

We perceive the space around us in a hemispherical way. But drawing involves reconstructing the scene on a flat surface, which creates distortions that increase the further we get from the center of our gaze (fig. 1).

Beyond 30° to either side of the direction of the gaze, the drawing will be stretched by 60% and will no longer be credible. Beyond 45°, the distortions will be on the order of 170% (fig. 2)!

It is generally recommended that we do not draw more than 30° to one side or the other of what we are looking at straight-on—in other words, we should stick to half of our binocular visual field (fig. 3).

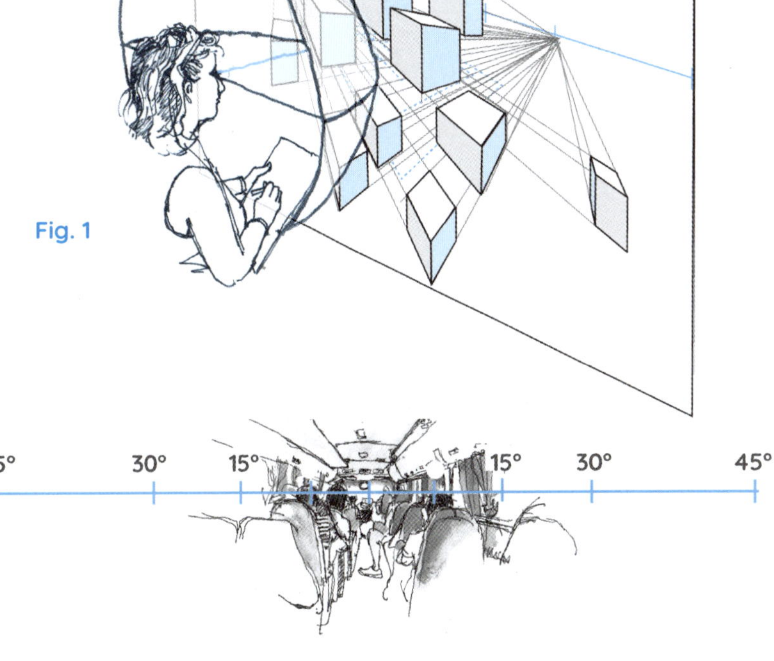

Fig. 1

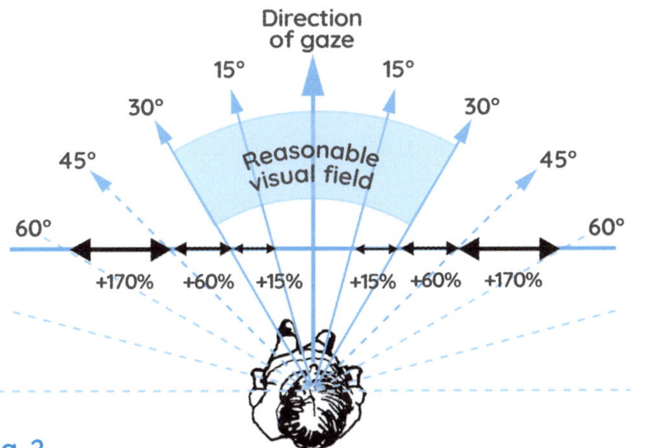

Fig. 2

Fig. 3   *Bus from Beirut to Sidon*

The Horizon

The Artist's Eyes

Let us assume that we look out horizontally. If I'm about 5'7", my eyes will be about 5 feet 3 inches from the ground. When I draw standing up, all of the eyes of the characters that are the same height as I am will line up along the horizontal line of my own eyes (fig. 1). The same is true for the landscape. Everything that is at the height of my eyes is along my horizon line (fig. 2).

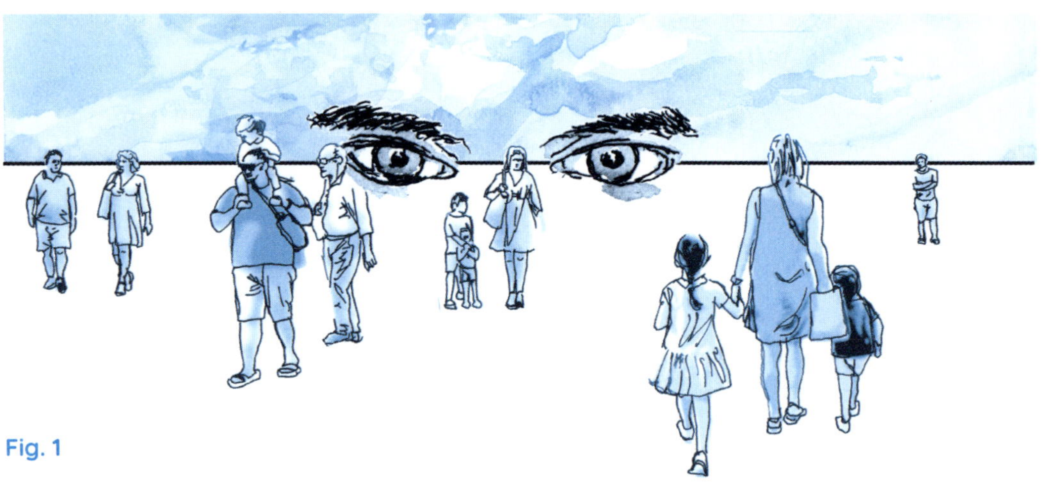

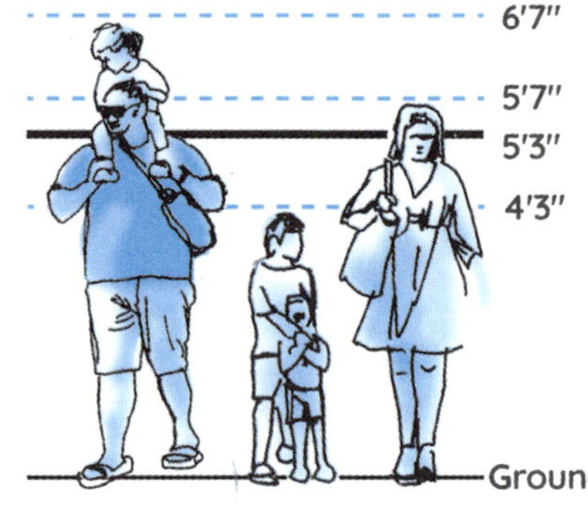

Fig. 1

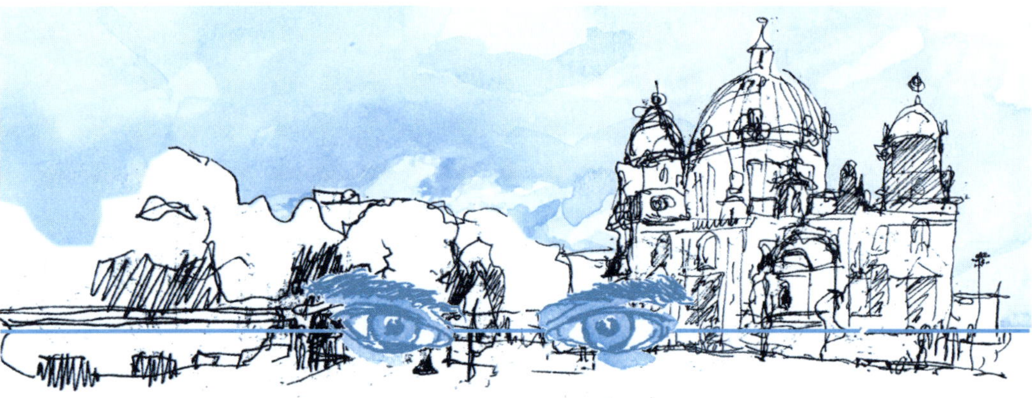

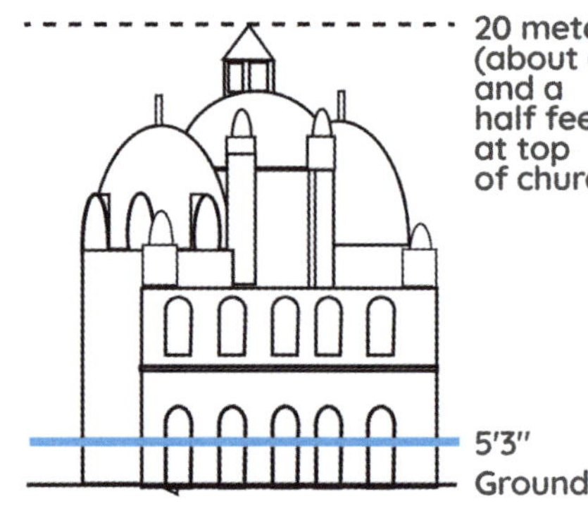

Fig. 2

Buildings are much taller than I am.

As a result, it becomes easy to position a character within a drawing, no matter how far away they are or what the setting is, by making all the elements coincide along my horizon line.

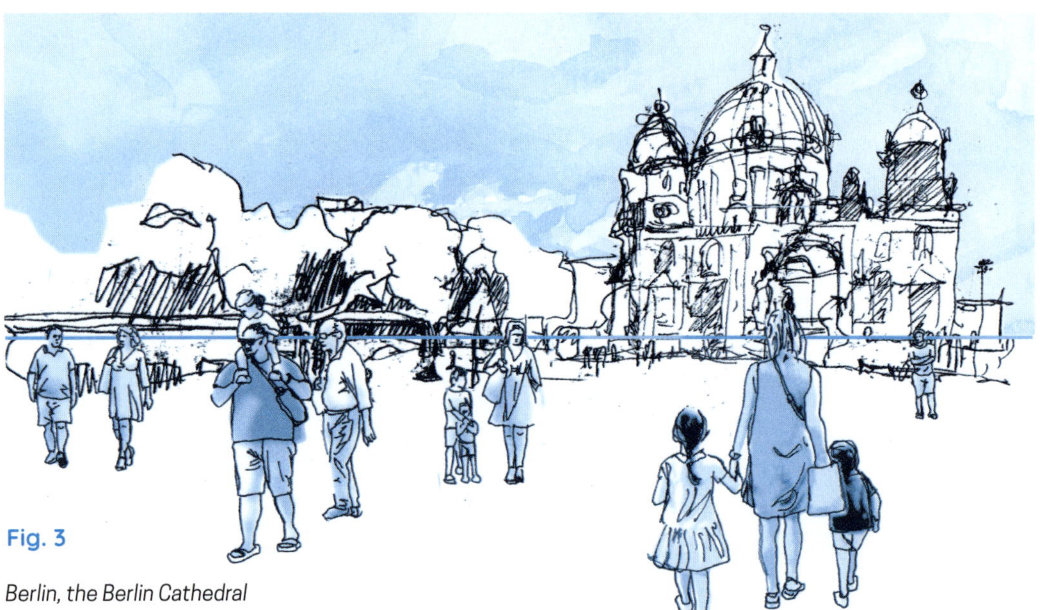

Fig. 3

Berlin, the Berlin Cathedral

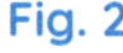

Horizon = Horizontal

Notice that the word "horizon" corresponds to what our eyes see along the horizontal level.

My horizon constitutes a reference point for all the heights in my drawing.

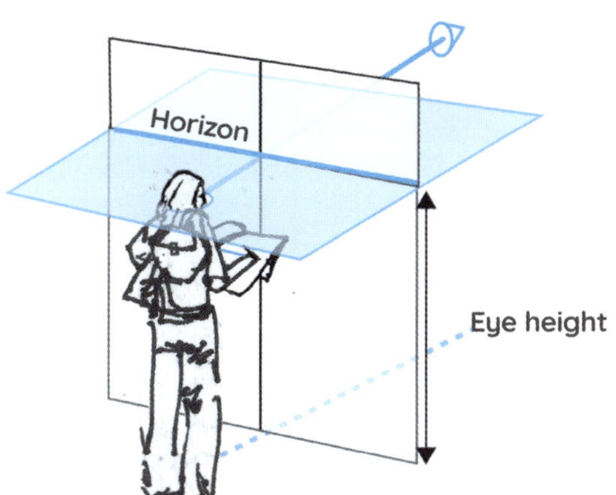

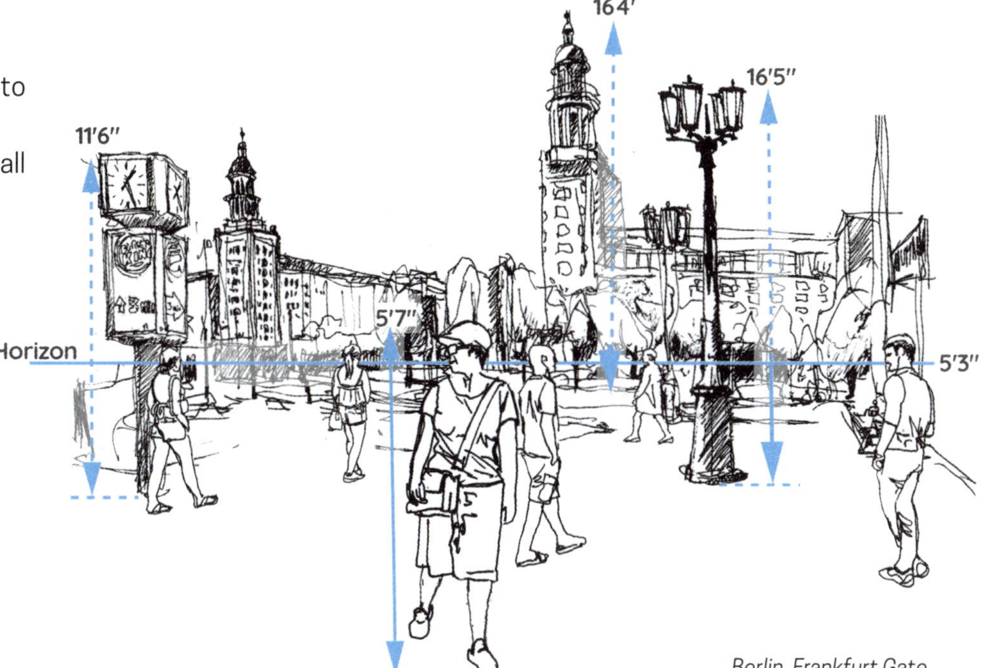

Berlin, Frankfurt Gate

Managing Your Point of View

In the image below, the eyes of the artist, when she is sitting down, are a little over 3 feet above the ground. Everything at this height will be aligned with her horizon (for instance, the navel of adult characters).

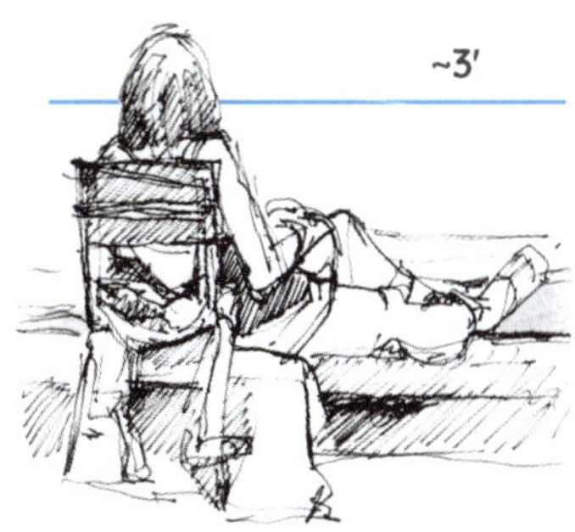

However tall I am, my horizon will always be at my eye level.

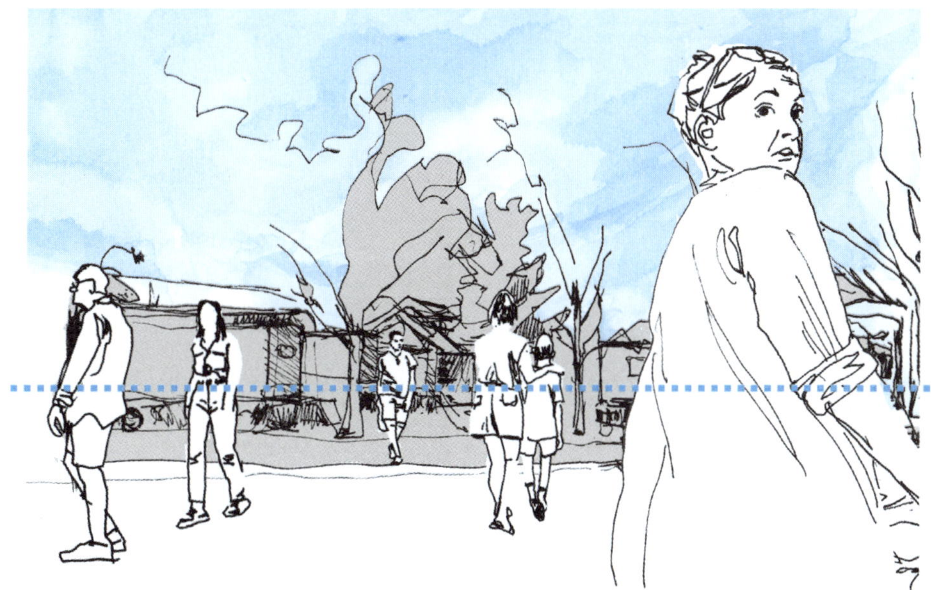

Vincennes, The Cartoucherie

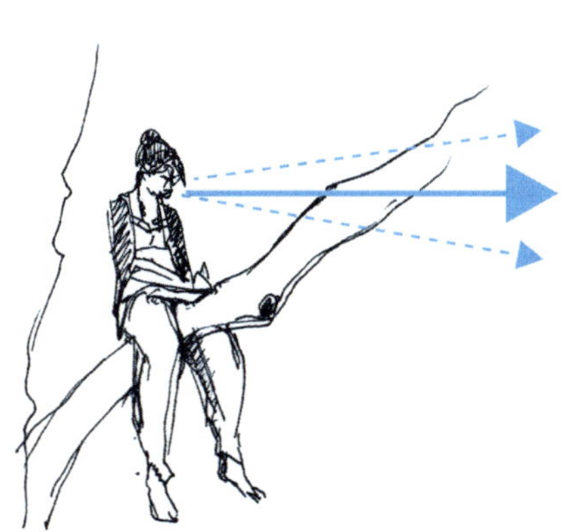

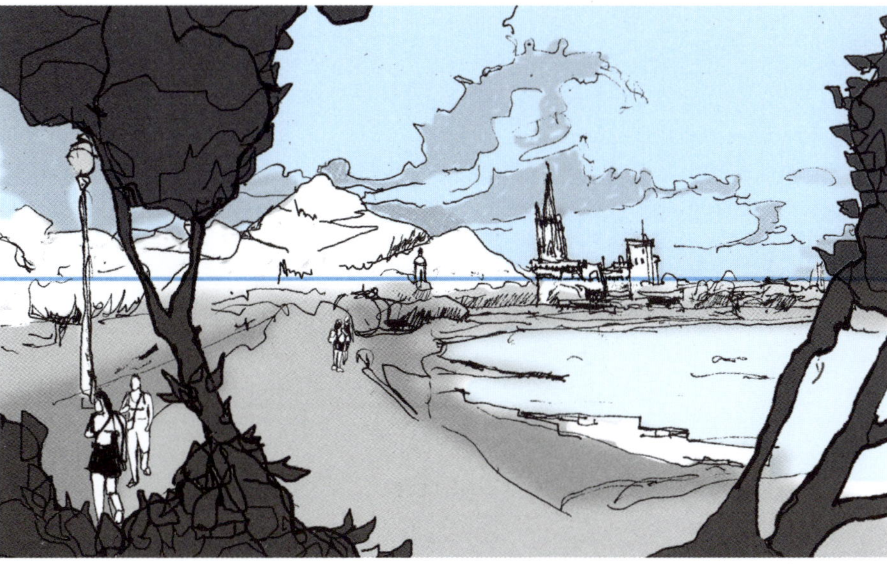

Vanishing Points

Directions and Convergences

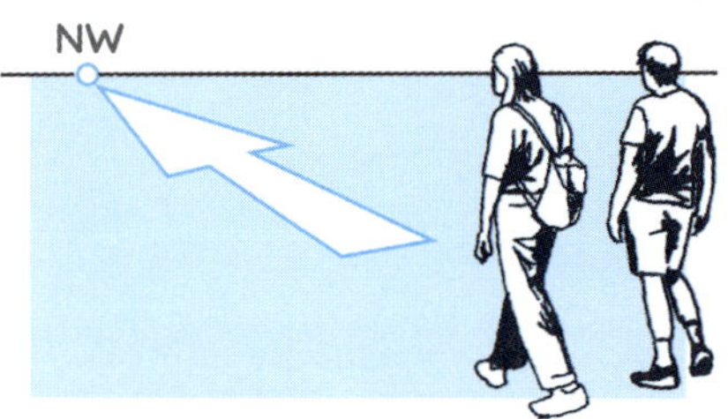

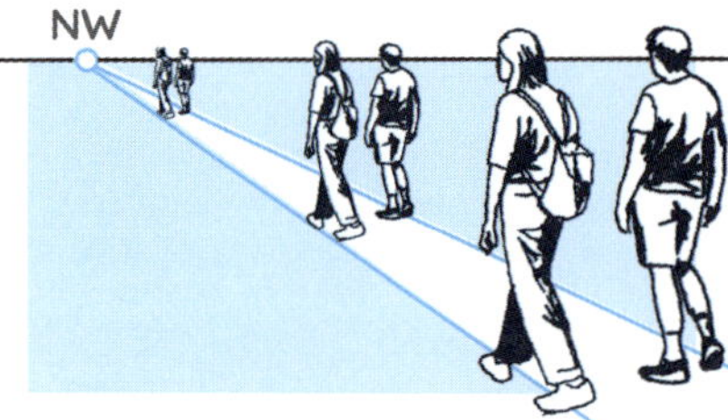

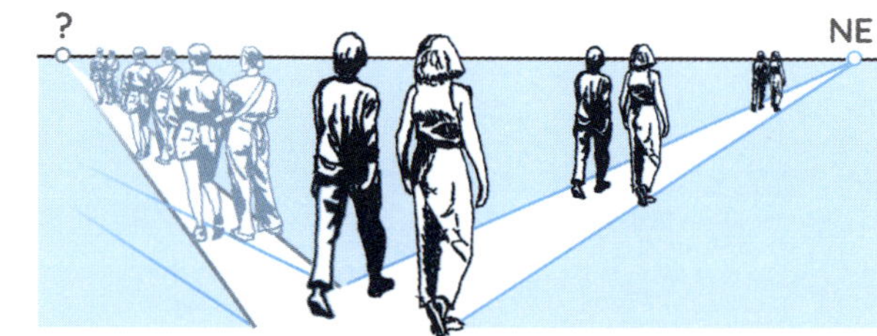

These two characters are heading northwest.

They are going in the same direction and will disappear into infinity at the same point.

Notice that they could also have gone northeast, or in any other direction.

All directions can be indicated by a point to my left, to my right, facing me. . . . We call these "**vanishing points**," the points toward which things vanish, or disappear.

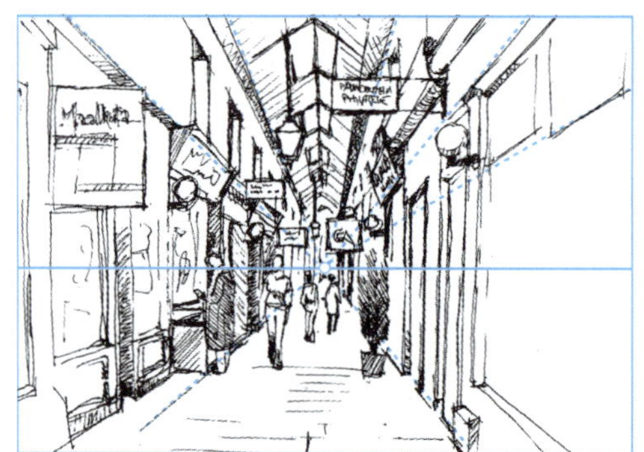

Paris, Passage des Panoramas (covered walkway)

Because the artist is looking toward the architecture here, the vanishing point will be at the center of their gaze.

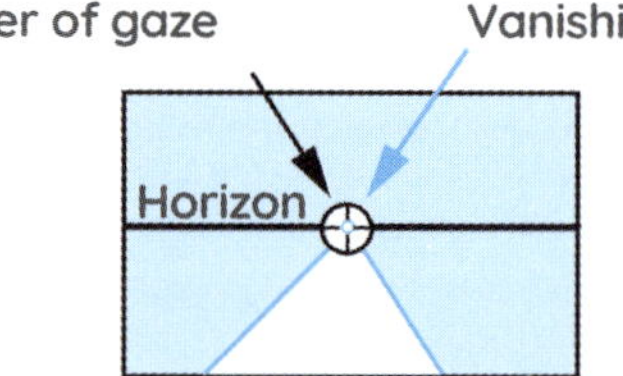

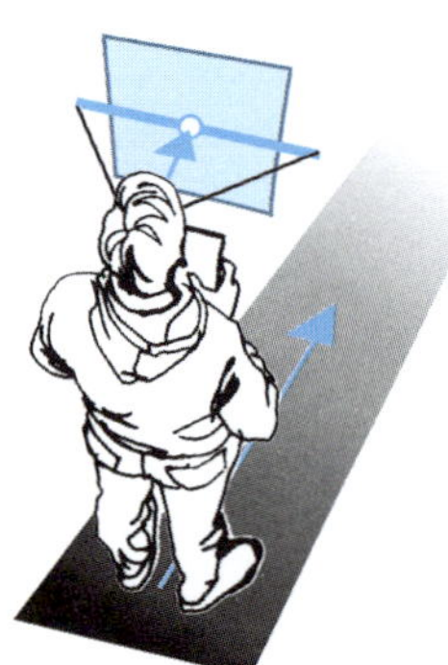

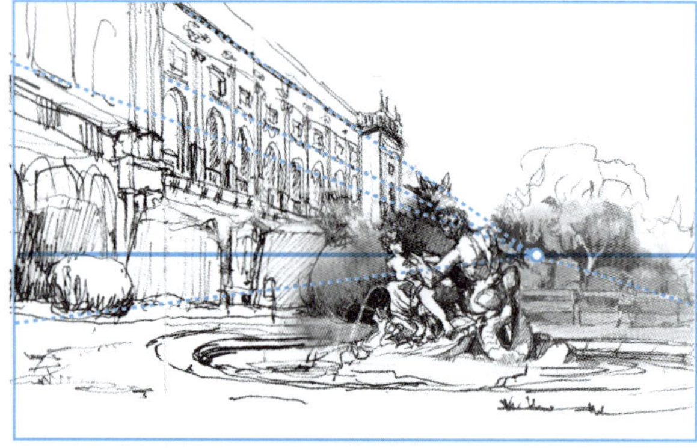

Vienna, Museum of Natural History

Here, the direction of the architecture (vanishing point) is slightly to the right of the center of the artist's gaze.

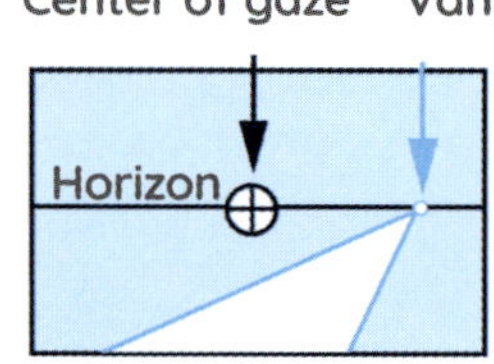

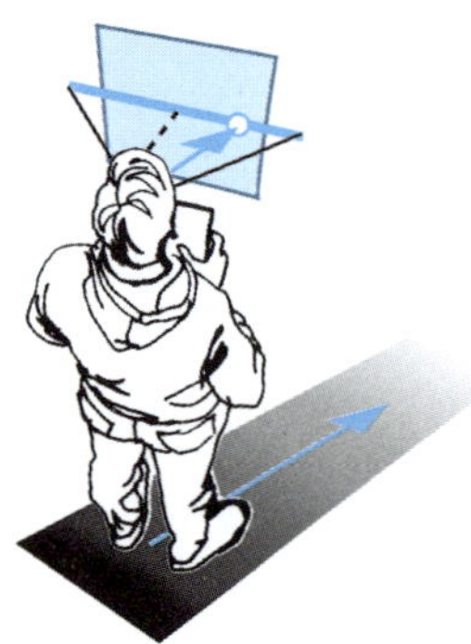

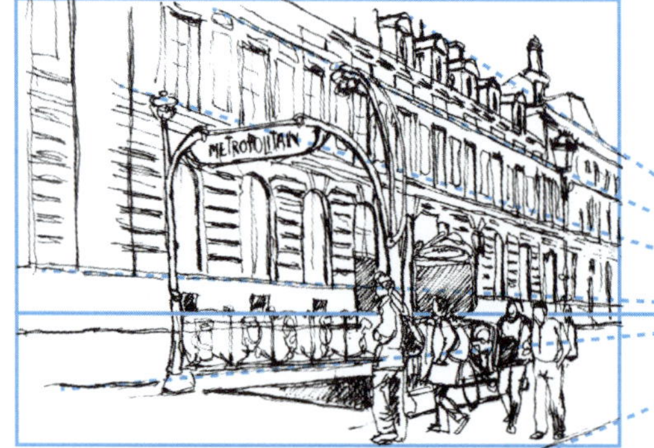

Paris, Louvre Museum

And here, finally, the direction of the architecture (vanishing point) is mostly alongside the area of the drawing.

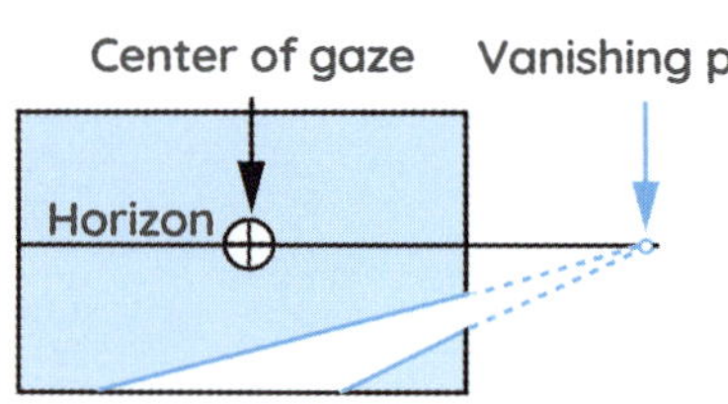

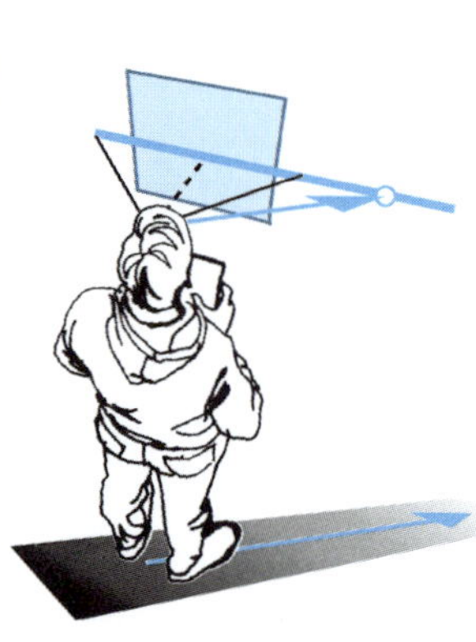

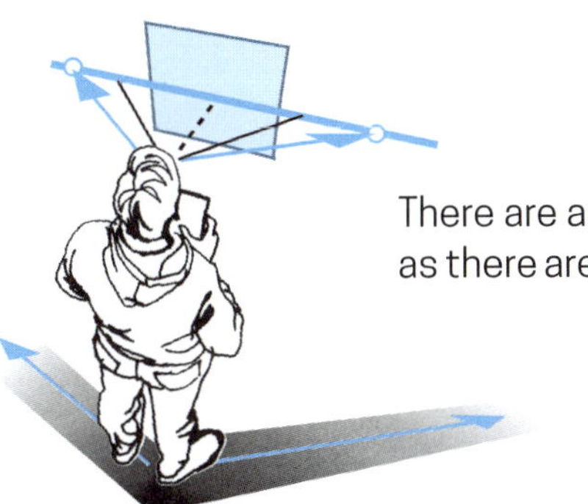

There are as many directions as there are vanishing points.

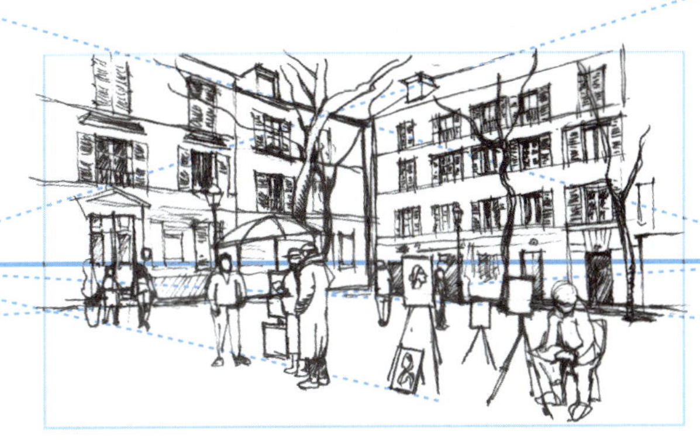

Paris, Montmartre, Place du Tertre

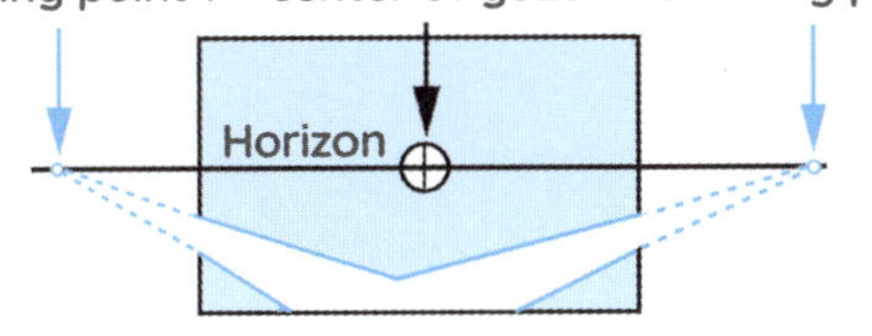

The center of the drawing (the center of the artist's vision) is completely independent of the direction of things in space.

All horizontal directions could be marked along the horizon line and become the subject of a specific vanishing point.

Below, I am looking to the north and I perceive all the directions of the space on either side of the center of my gaze.

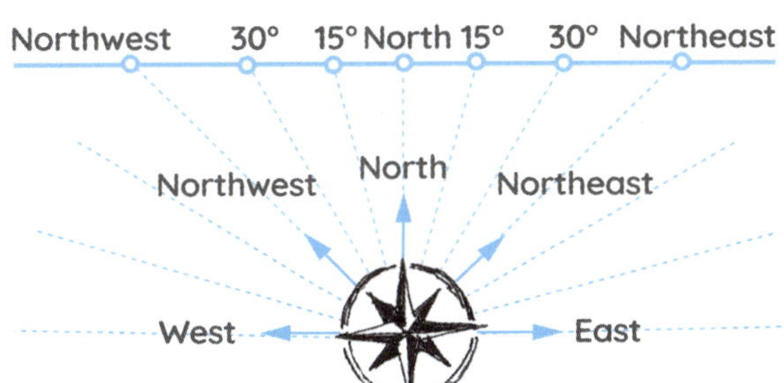

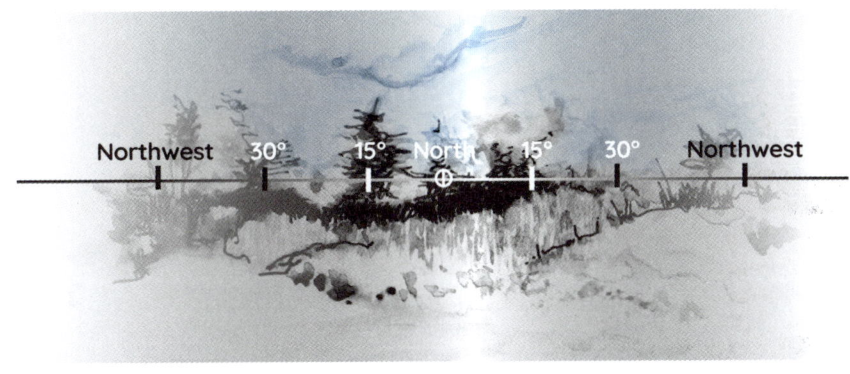

Saint-Brevin, in the dunes

Placing the Vanishing Points

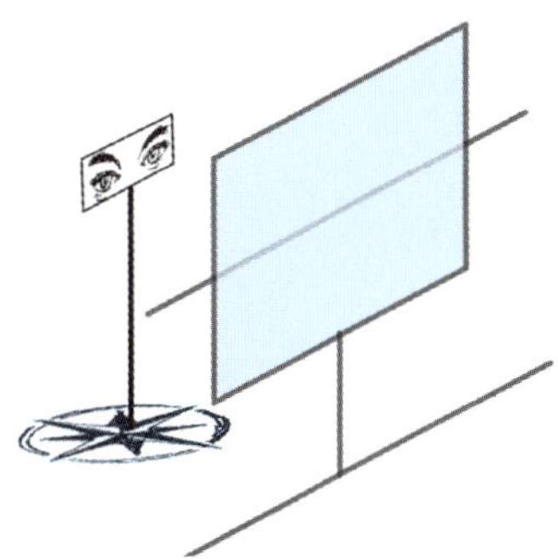

1. Locate your horizon and identify the area of your drawing.

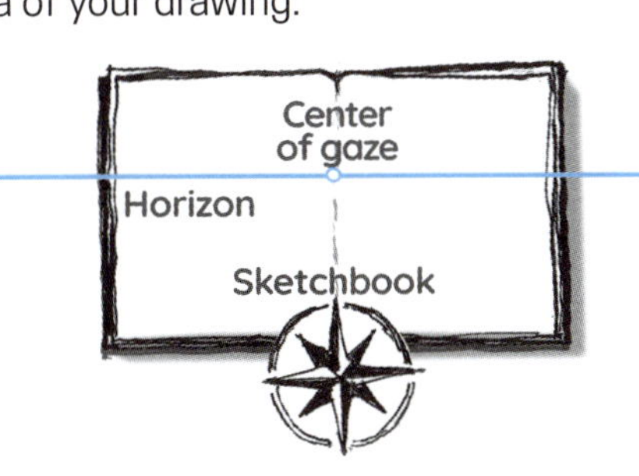

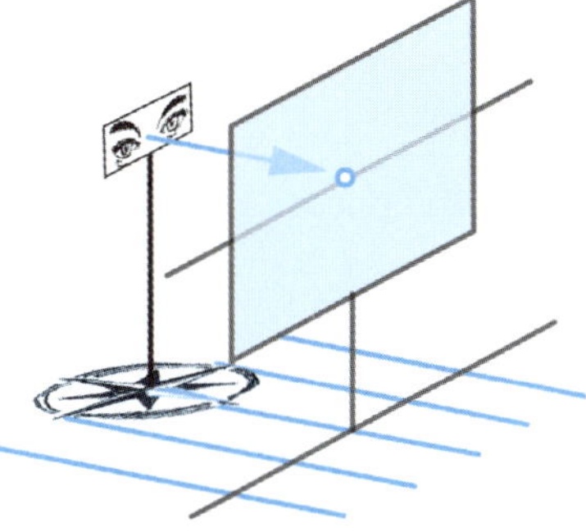

2. Locate the primary direction of the space.

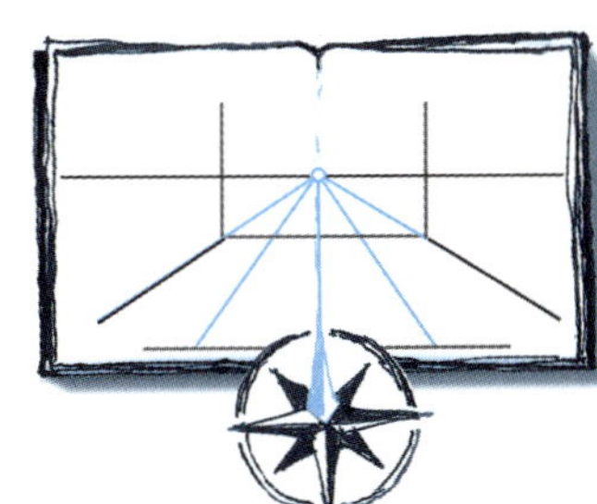

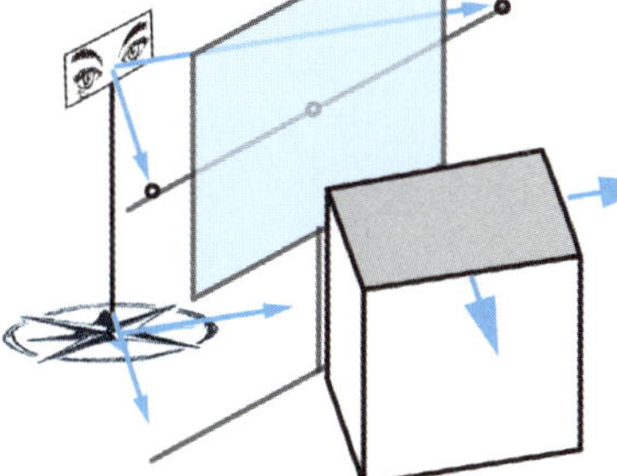

3. Locate the auxiliary directions.

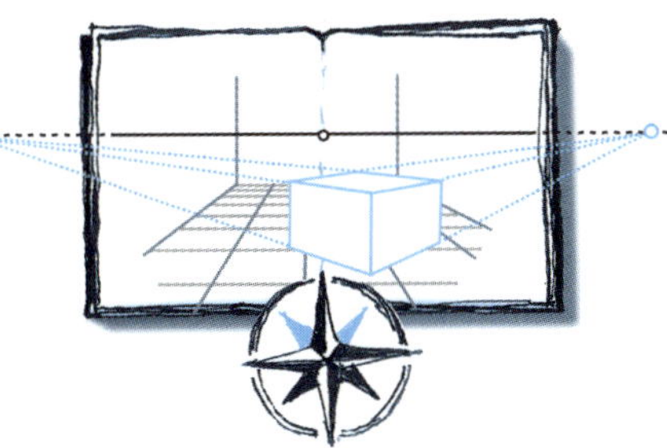

Perceived Space

Space is defined in three dimensions: height, width, and depth. But the artist perceives it according to where their eyes are located and according to the direction of their gaze. Thus, it will be more accurate to define space according to three planes—the horizontal, the sagittal (or median), and the frontal—along which the vanishing points can be perceived.

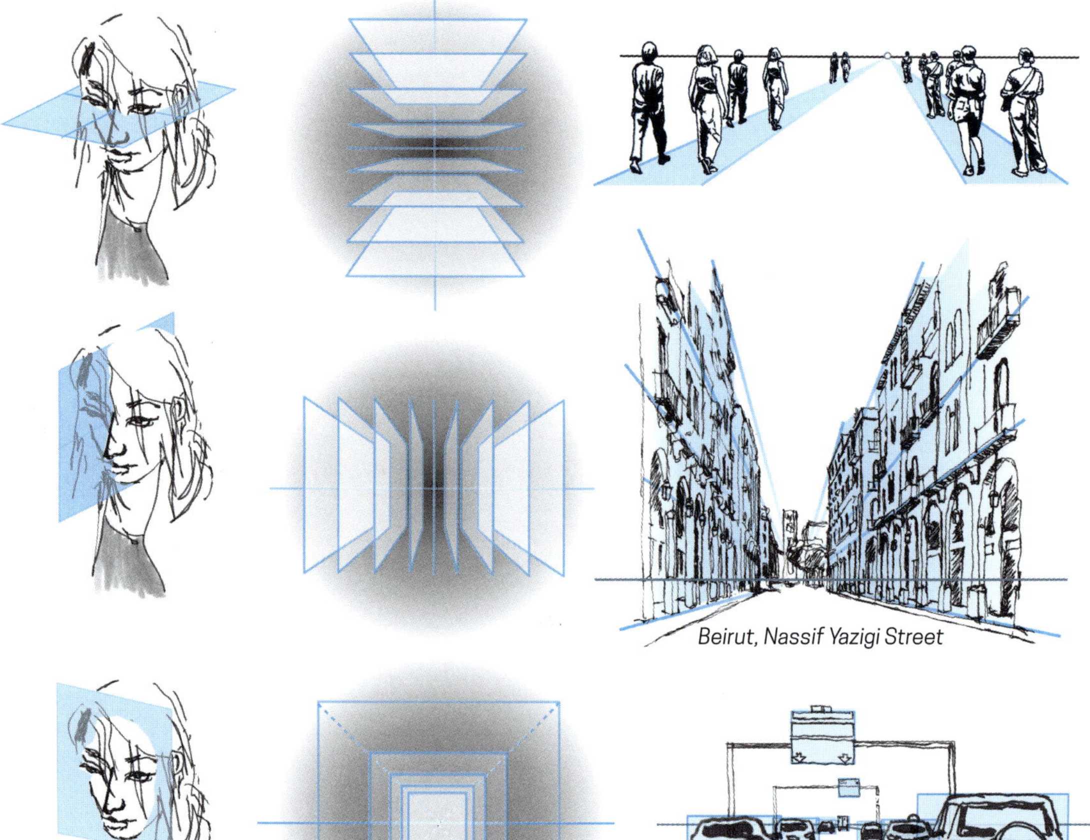

The **horizontal** plane separates above from below with respect to our eyes. Note that drawings are usually busier and fuller below our eyes (for instance, on the ground) and airier above them (the sky).

The **sagittal** or median plane separates left from right. Our brain synthesizes what our two eyes see. Where these two sides meet is the direction of our gaze.

Beirut, Nassif Yazigi Street

The **frontal** plane, parallel with our face, separates front from back. Objects shrink as they move farther away from us, but they keep the same proportions.

From Top to Bottom

The notions of the visual field, the horizon, and the vanishing point are all completely linked with each other. They make it possible for us to juggle with space from top to bottom, left to right, and near and far.

Even though we perceive equal amounts of space above and below our horizontal gaze, we can shift our composition based on our zone of interest. However, do pay attention to the distortions!

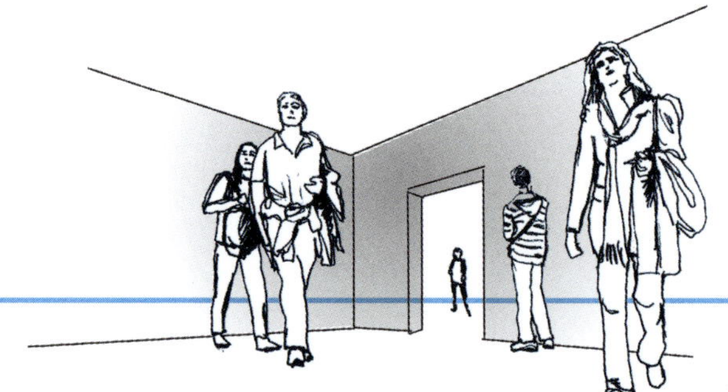

Here, the artist is sitting on the ground, at the height of the characters' knees.

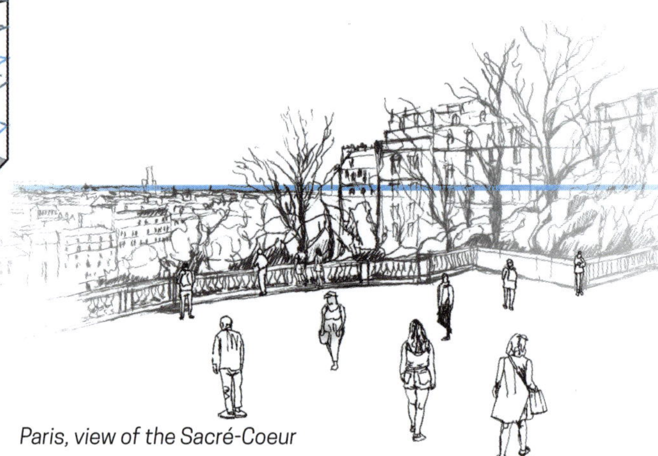

Paris, view of the Sacré-Coeur

Here, on the other hand, the artist is towering over them from two and a half times their height.

From Left to Right

To position the vanishing points correctly, knowing that there are as many of them as there are directions, we have to locate these before we start drawing.

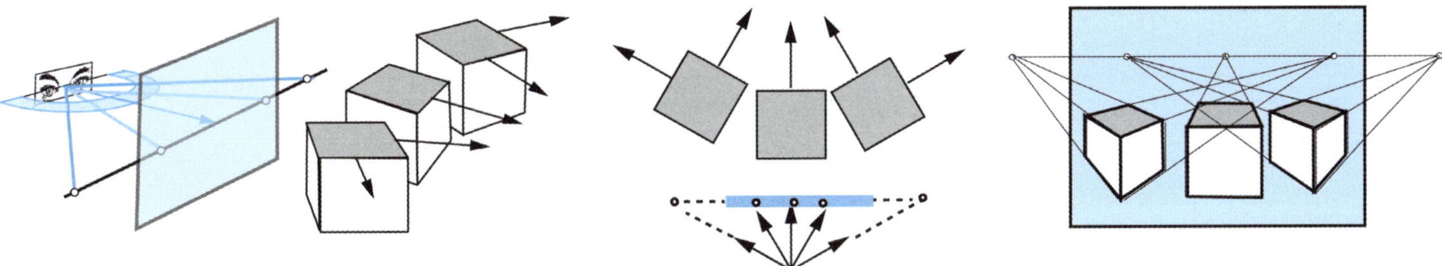

From Up Close and Far Away

The vanishing points must be separated from each other according to the distance from which we are observing them.

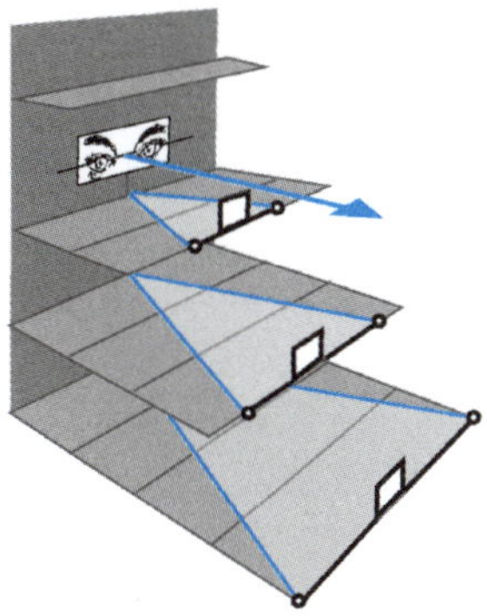

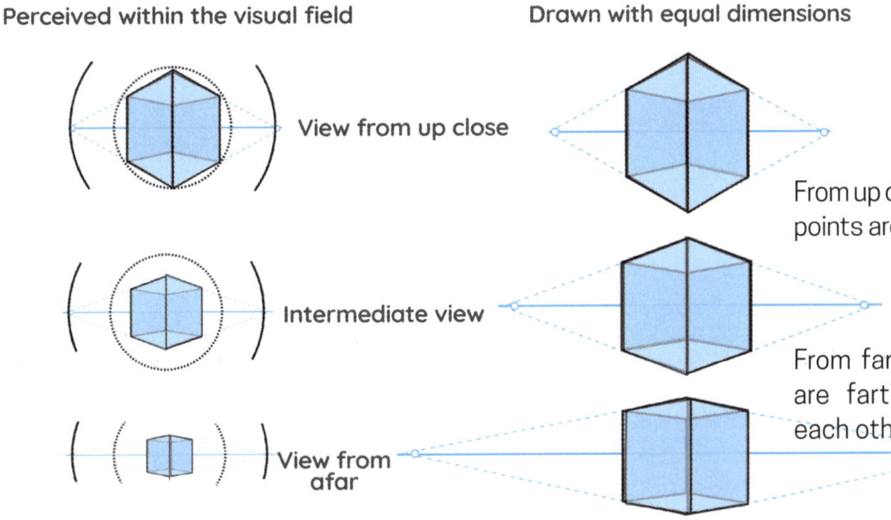

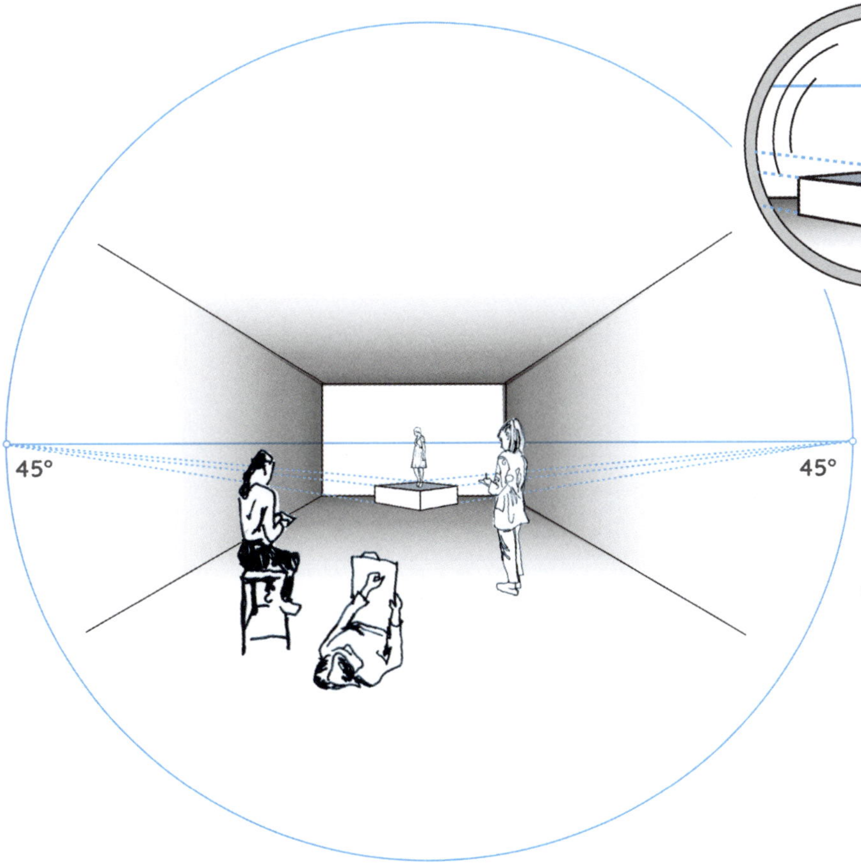

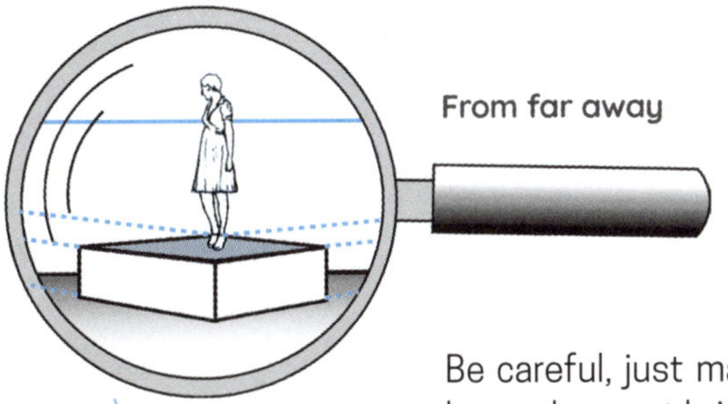

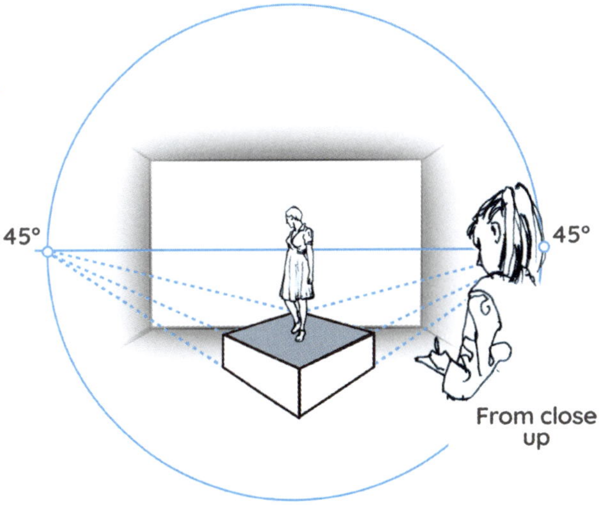

Right Angles

Right angles are omnipresent in space and in our perception. Knowing how to reproduce them will allow us to draw a coherent three-dimensional space.

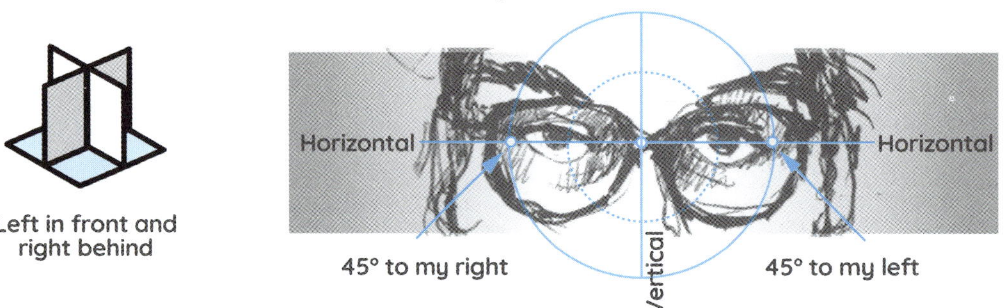

Left in front and
right behind

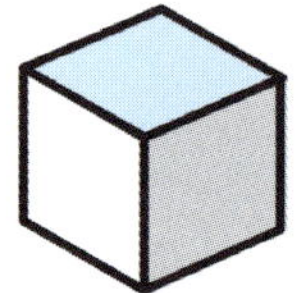

Height, width, depth

At the Intersection of Two Dimensions

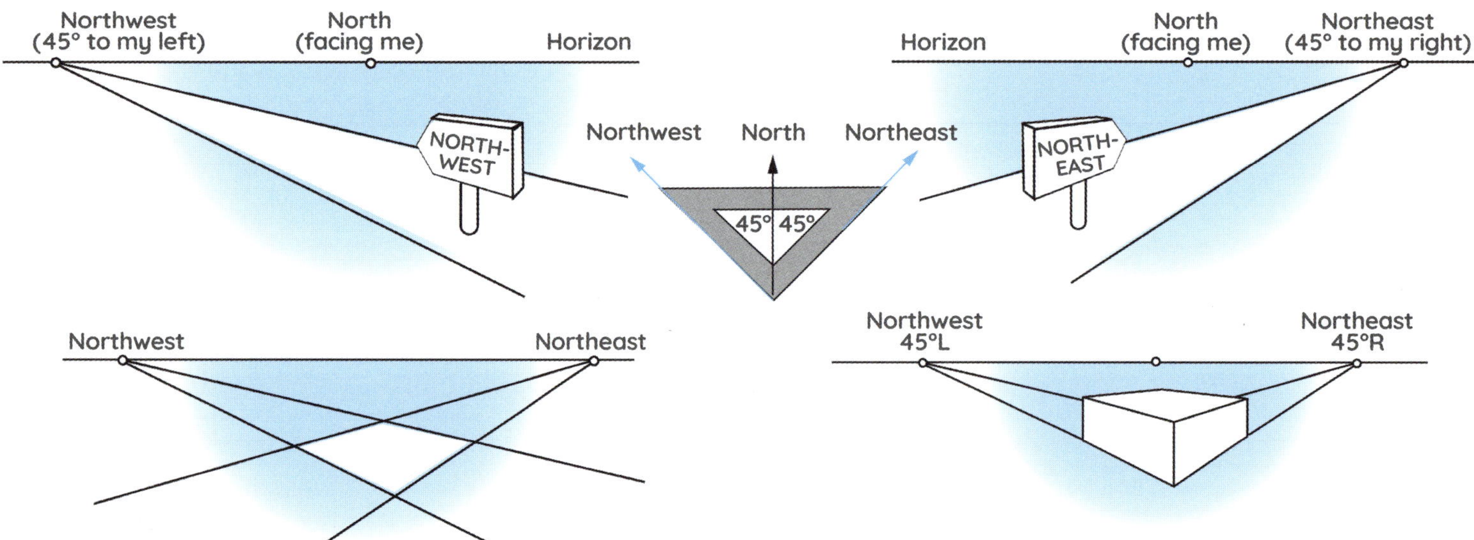

At the intersection of these two paths, we will obtain a rectangle. But note that four right angles do not necessarily form a square . . .

These two angular benchmarks will form the yardstick for our vision in perspective. We will call these directions **45L** (45° to my left) and **45R** (45° to my right).

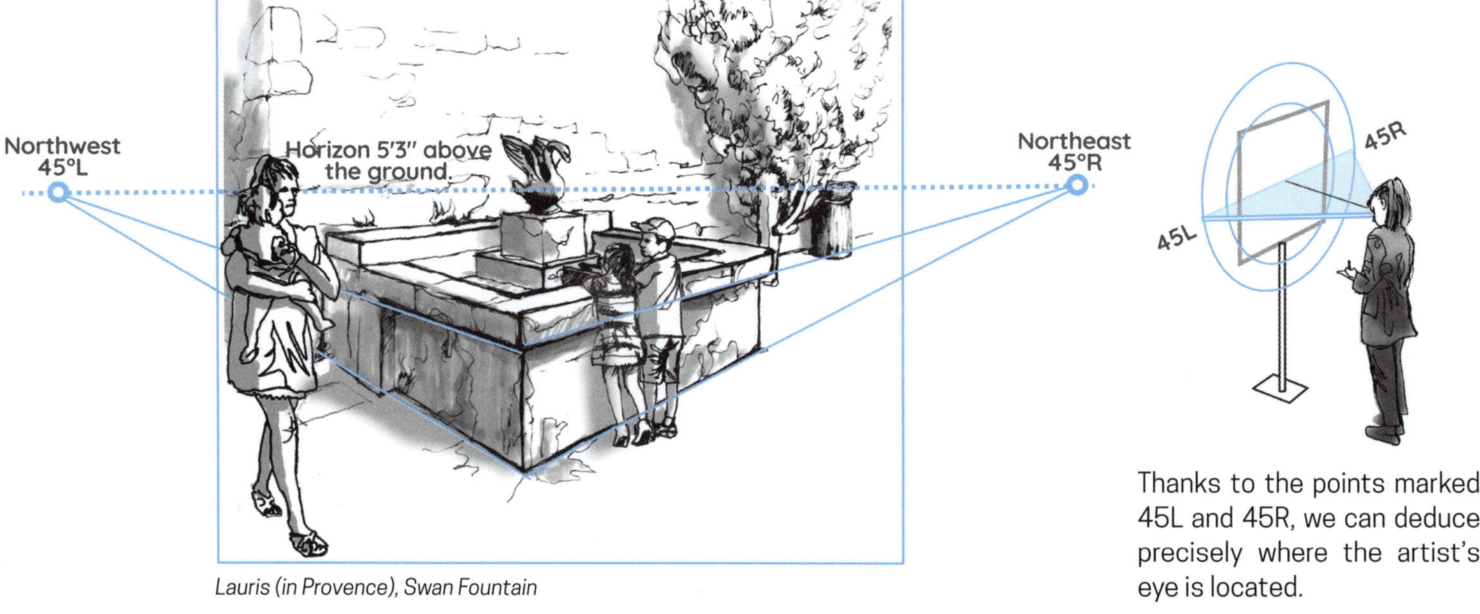

Lauris (in Provence), Swan Fountain

Thanks to the points marked 45L and 45R, we can deduce precisely where the artist's eye is located.

The Artist's Eye

We have seen that our eye can determine the position of all the directions of space. This will turn out to be very practical for establishing precise angles (fig. 1). But our eye is not **inside** the drawing. It is **in front of** the page, facing the center (fig. 2). Still, we can use the geometric concept of triangulation to simulate the directions by tilting the artist's eye onto the drawing, which amounts to the same thing, geometrically (fig. 3). Starting from this position, which we will call **EP** (the eye of perspective), we will be able to position the vanishing points wherever we want to (90° of difference between two points = a right angle; fig. 4).

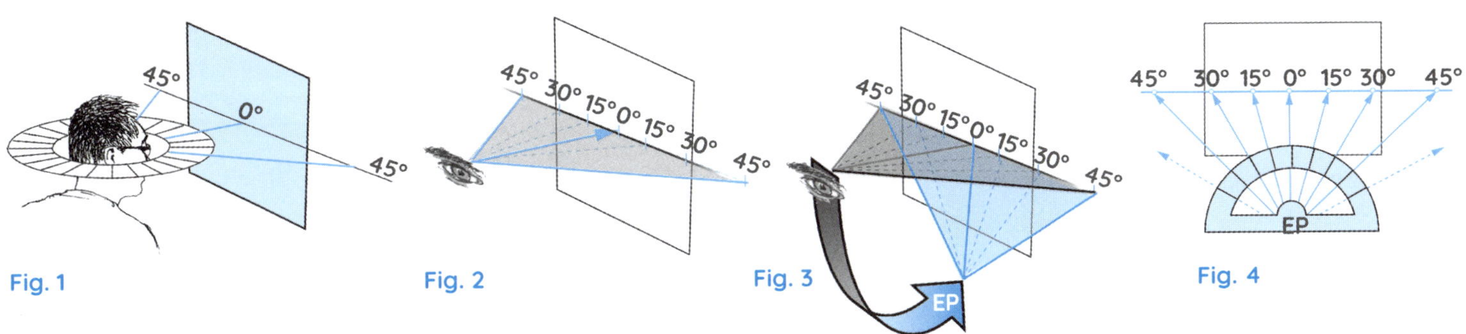

Here are two methods for positioning EP, this strategic position that is particularly important for our future constructions, on the basis of a previously defined visual field (setting the directions at 45° on either side).

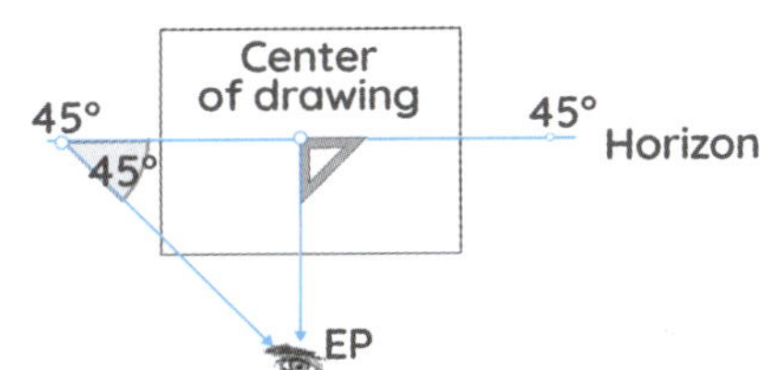

Solution 1: From one of the 45° points, descend at a 45° angle down to the central axis.

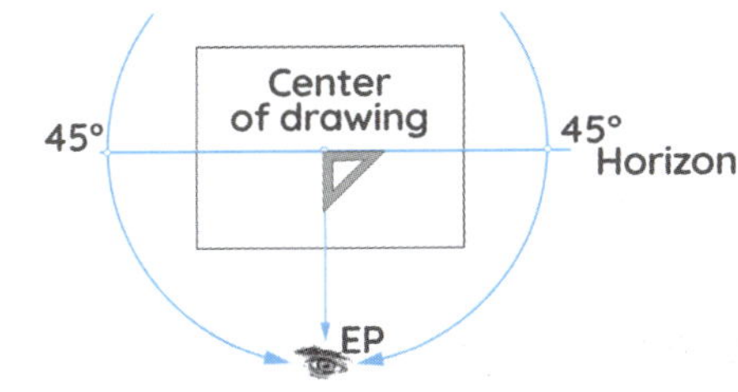

Solution 2: Draw a circle starting at the center and passing through the 45° points.

Constructing Right Angles

This bench is oriented exactly in the directions pointing at 45°.

We can find pairs of directions at right angles to each other by simply tilting a triangle tool with its right-angle base located at EP. Note that, inversely, we can also position EP within the central axis of the drawing starting from any two directions that form a right angle.

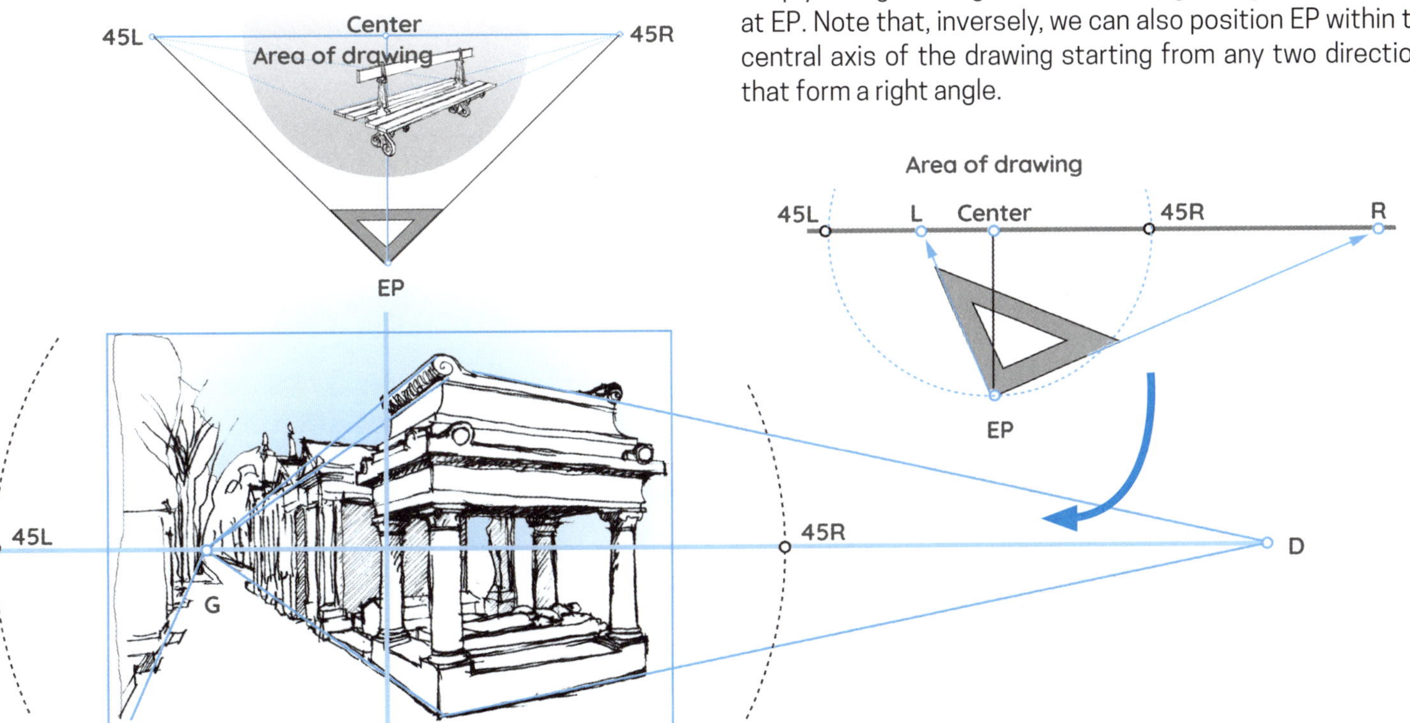

Paris, Montmartre cemetery, Alexandre Dumas's tomb

Slopes

When a surface is sloped, it only changes direction from top to bottom. A sloped surface thus has a vanishing point that is located above its horizontal direction if it is tilted upward, and below it if it is tilted downward.

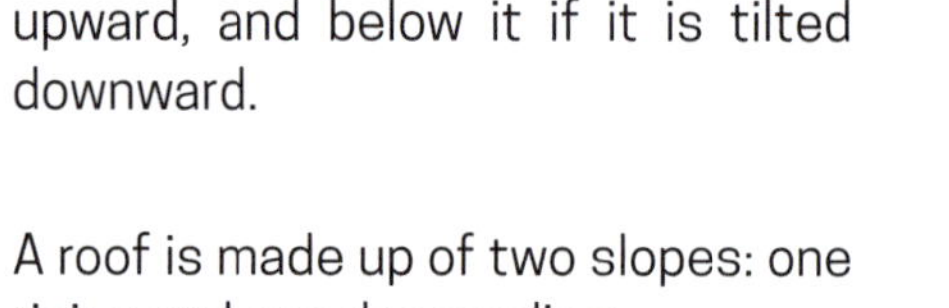

A roof is made up of two slopes: one rising and one descending.

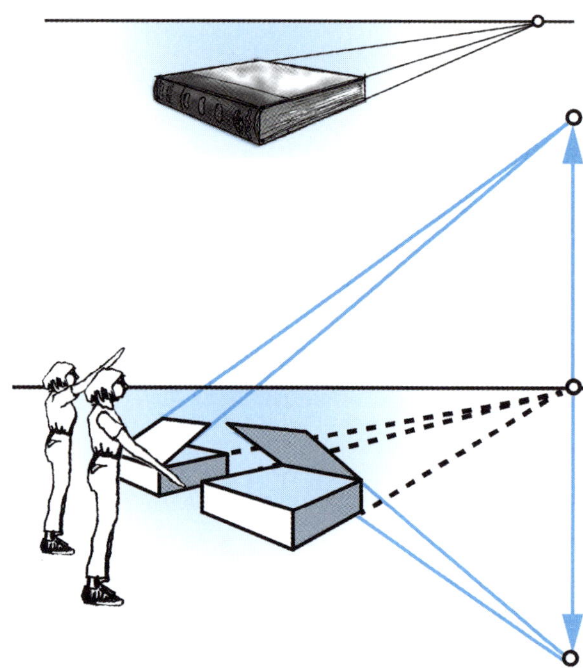

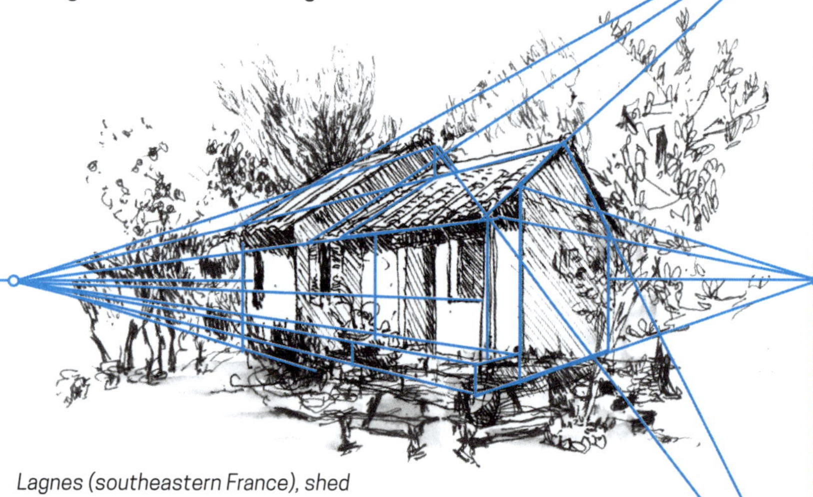

Lagnes (southeastern France), shed

A rising or descending slope? This is a question of your point of view. Extend your arm parallel to the slope and you will know whether it is rising or descending!

Descending Slope

The vanishing point of a street that is descending will be below the horizon, while the architectural elements (which are horizontal!) will continue to be directed toward the horizon.

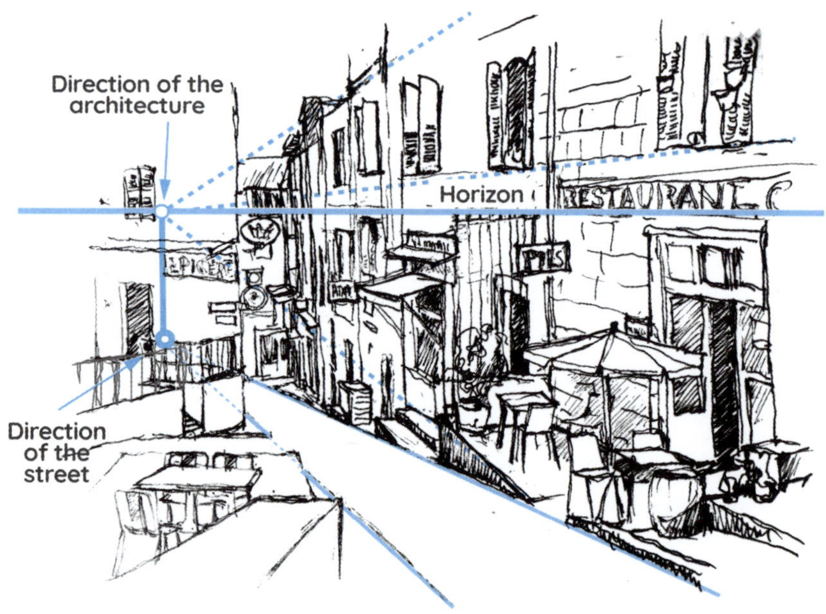

Rising Slope

If the street is rising, its vanishing point will be located above the horizon. The architectural elements will keep their horizontal directions, as always.

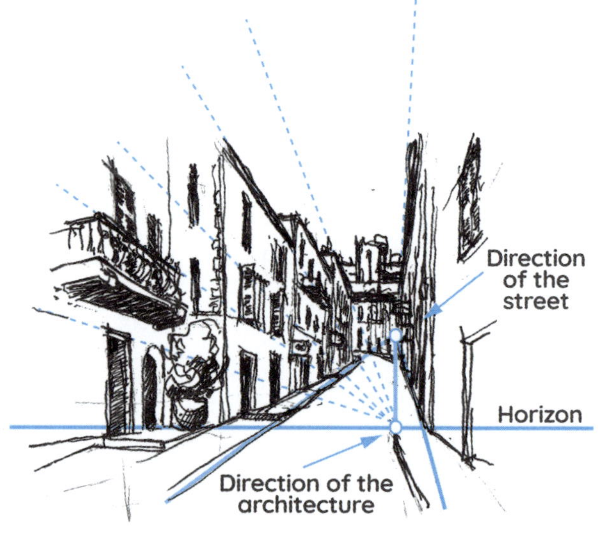

Calculating the Degree of the Slope

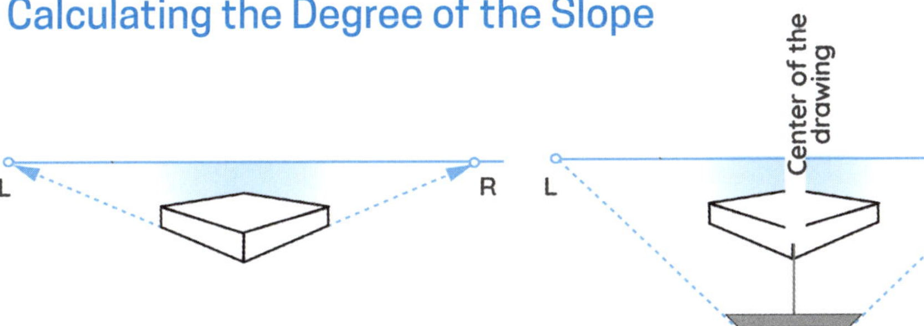

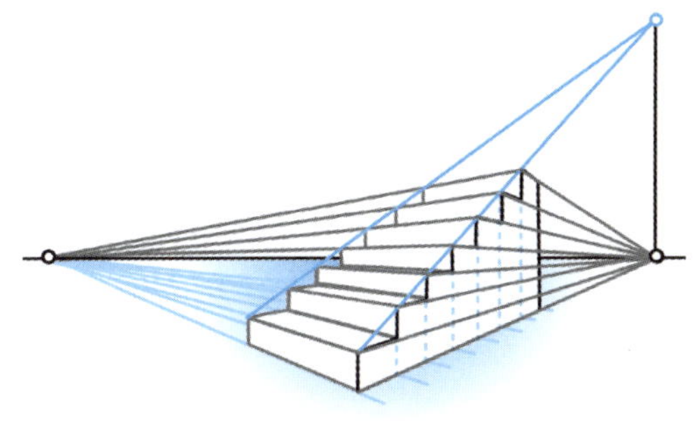

1. Locate two horizontal directions that make a right angle.

2. Place point EP in the central axis of the drawing (see **The Artist's Eye**, p. 13).

A staircase is made up of a succession of horizontal and vertical surfaces along a slope of between 25° and 45°.

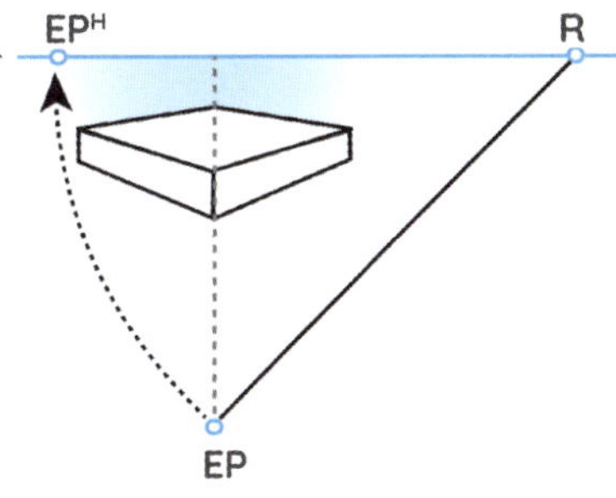

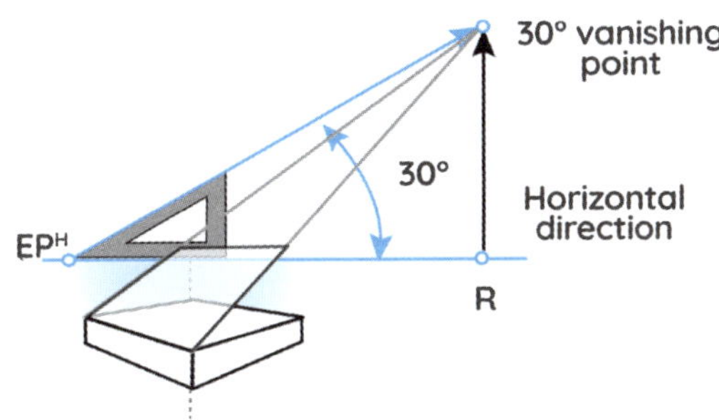

3. Using a compass, take the distance EP–R (distance from the eye of perspective to point R on the right-hand side along the direction of the slope) and draw it along the horizon line to find the point EP^H.

4. Starting from point EP^H, draw the desired slope upward to the plumb-up line from point R (which shows the direction of the slope).

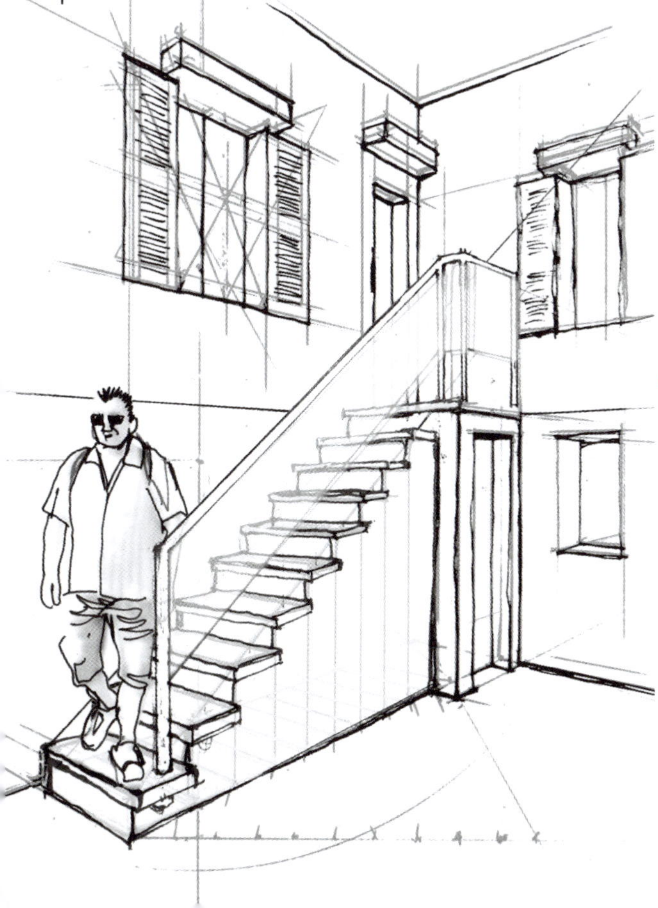

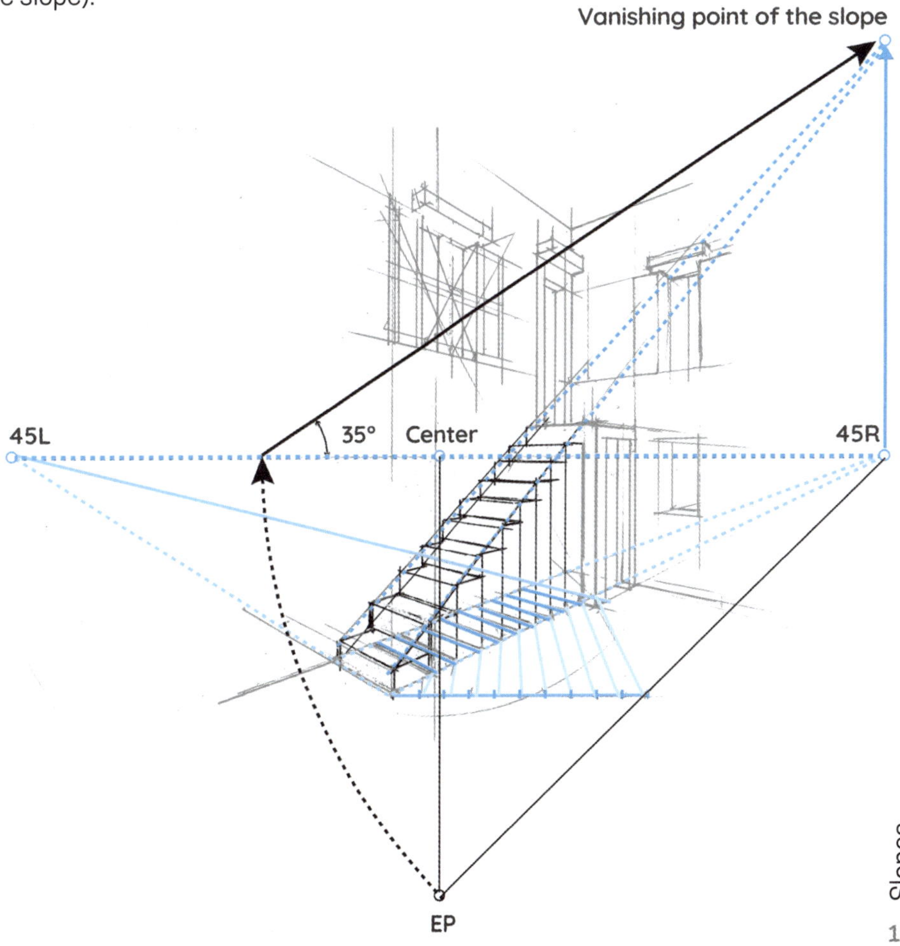

Triangulation

Copying a distance, creating multiple copies of an element of the background or setting, finding the center, creating a geometric whole: these are all situations that we can resolve using the principle of geometric triangulation.

In this example, we are going to duplicate a surface in a given direction. We can consider three different possibilities.

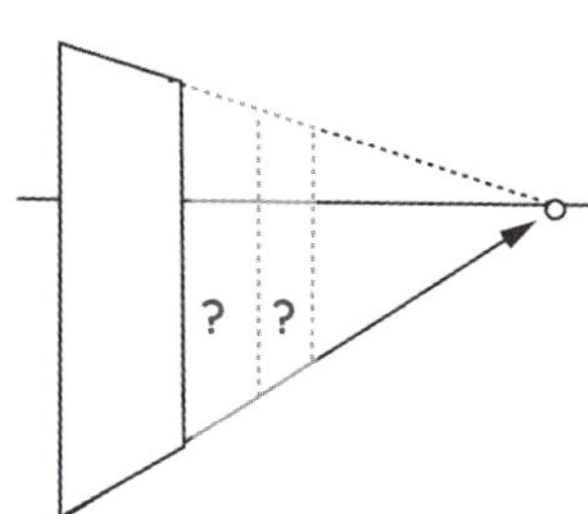

Geometric Copying

1. Divide the entire surface into two equal sections.
2. Go from one corner to the following center in order to copy the distance.

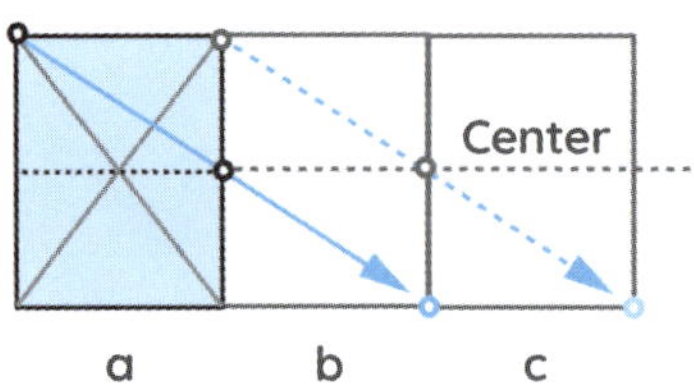

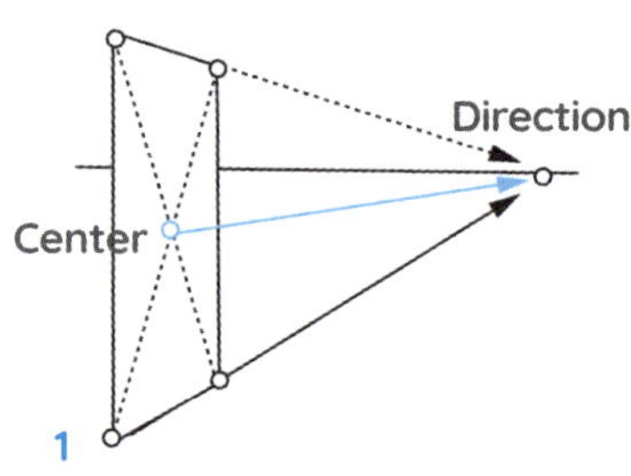

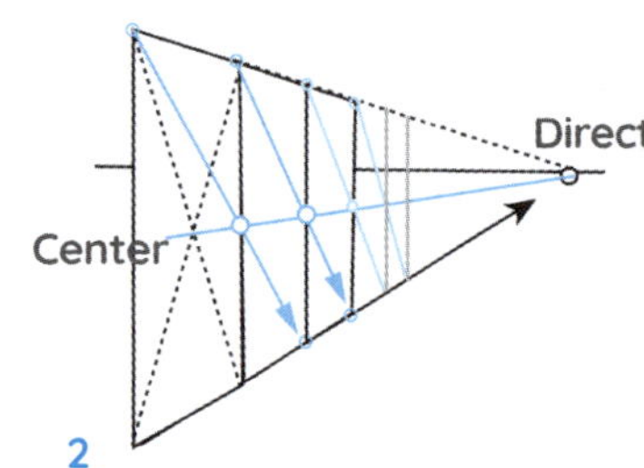

Frontal Copying

1. Enclose the first distance within a frontal corridor of known dimension (0–1).
2. Multiply these corridors to find the intersection points.

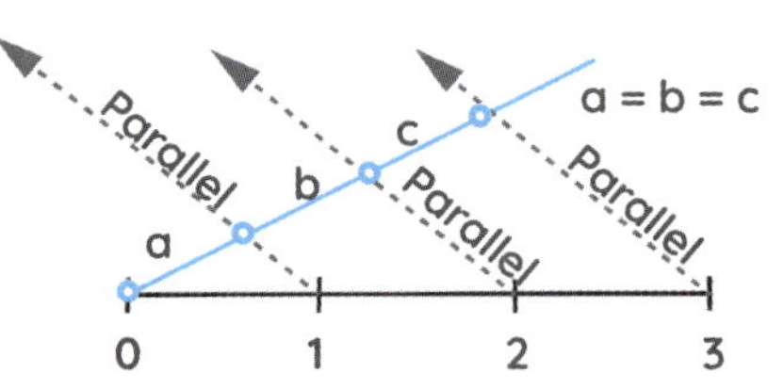

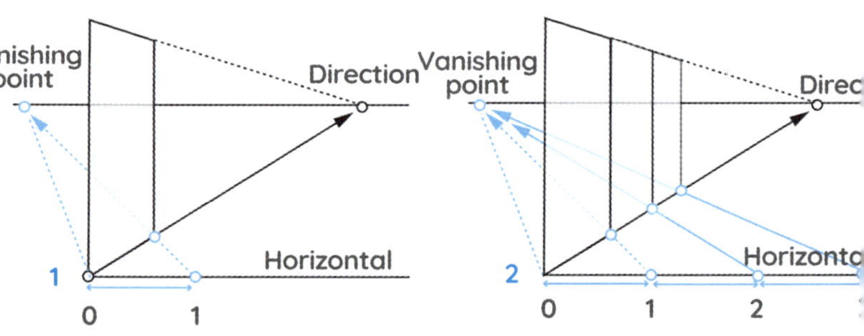

Slope Copying

1. Extend the diagonal of the first measurement in order to find its slope (see **Slopes**, p. 14).
2. Follow the same slope for the following measurements.

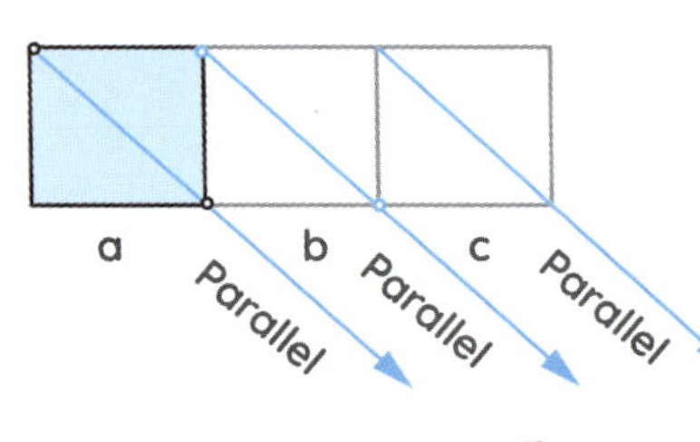

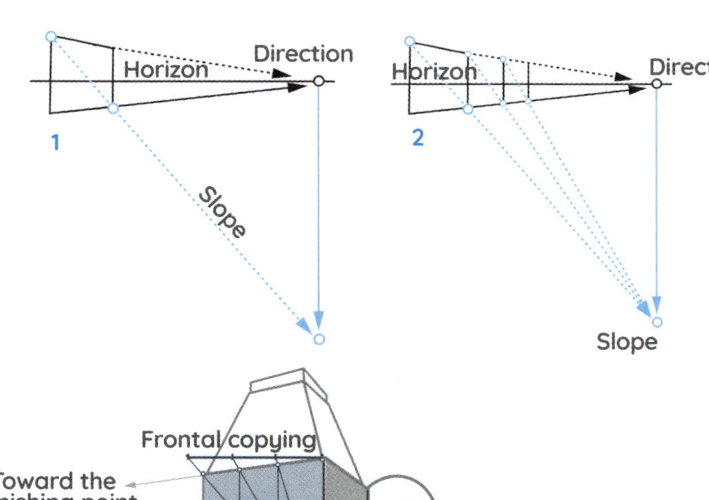

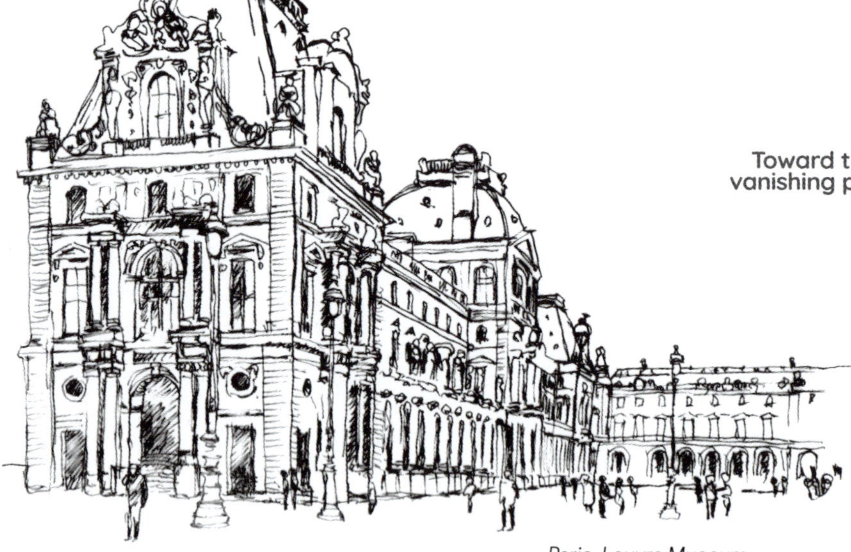

Paris, Louvre Museum

The Diagonal

The diagonal is an essential element for triangulation in geometric constructions. Below you will find the procedure for making sure you are drawing a square on the horizontal plane, and then raising it vertically to obtain a cube.

Implementation of frontal and diagonal triangulation:

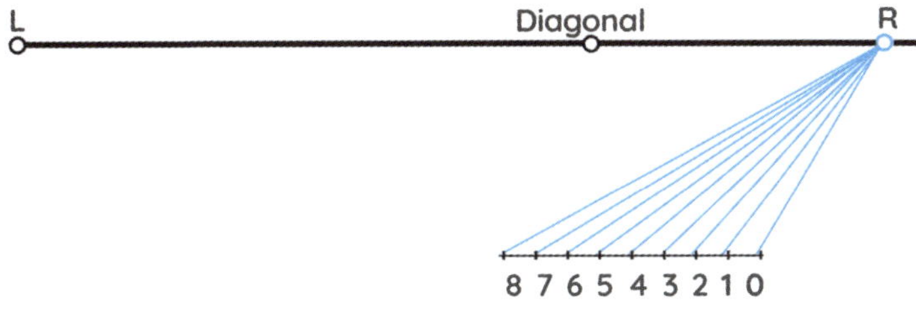

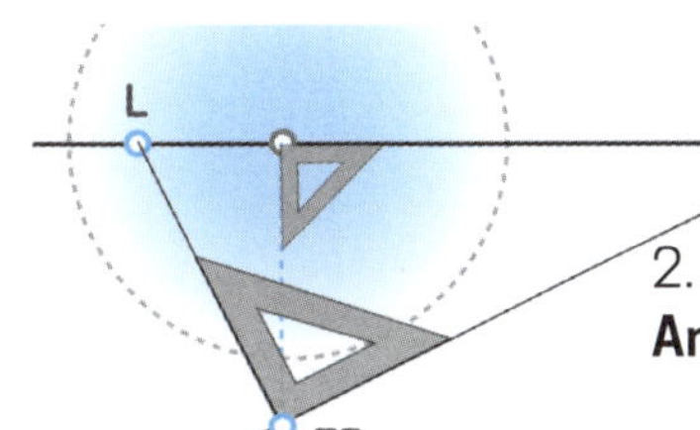

1. Position the two vanishing points that form a right angle.

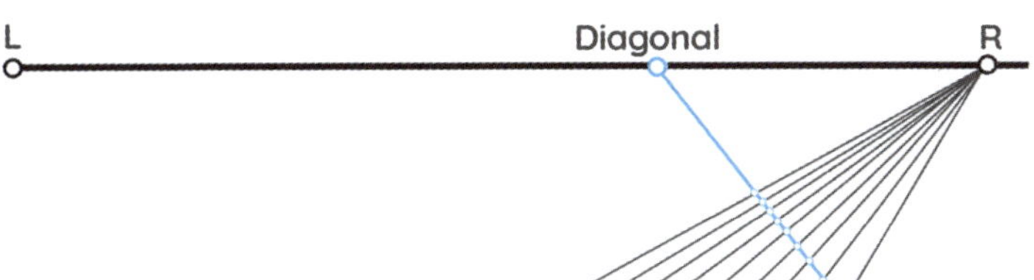

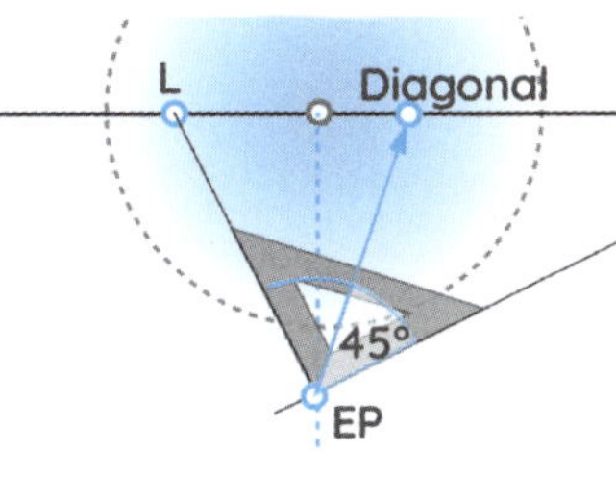

2. Find point EP (see **Right Angles**, p. 13).

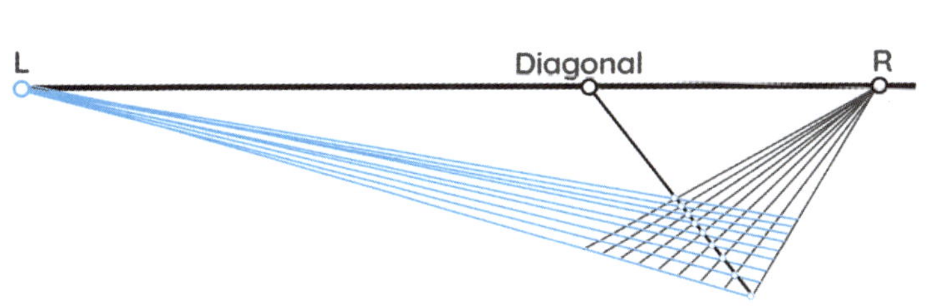

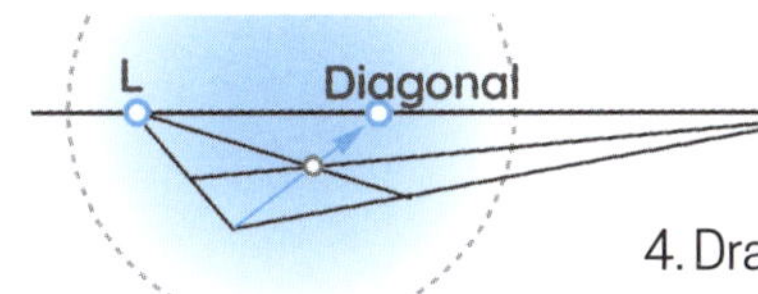

3. Position the vanishing point of the diagonals starting from EP (at a 45° angle in each direction).

4. Draw a square on the ground.

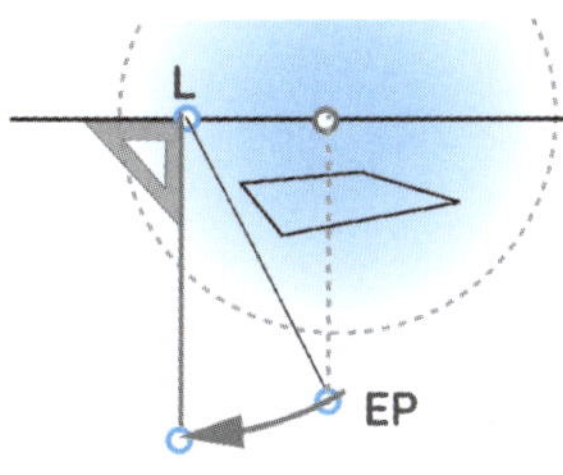

5. Find the vanishing point at 45° on the left (see **Slopes**, p. 15).

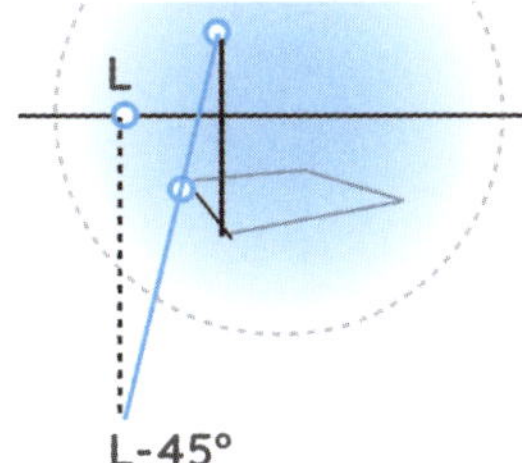

6. Use a geometric triangulation to find a height equivalent to the depth of the square.

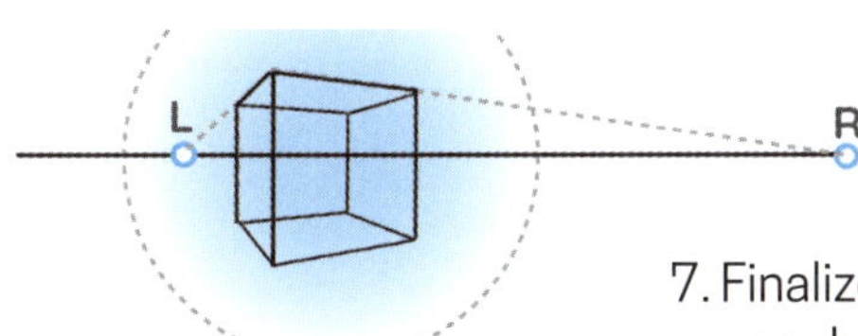

7. Finalize the construction of your cube.

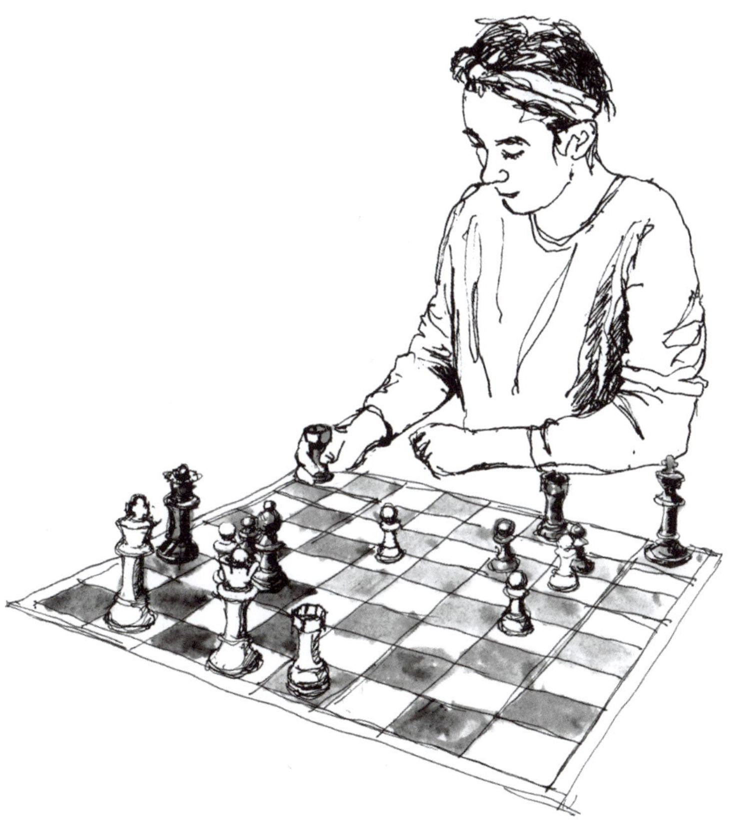

White will checkmate in four moves

Measurements

Height

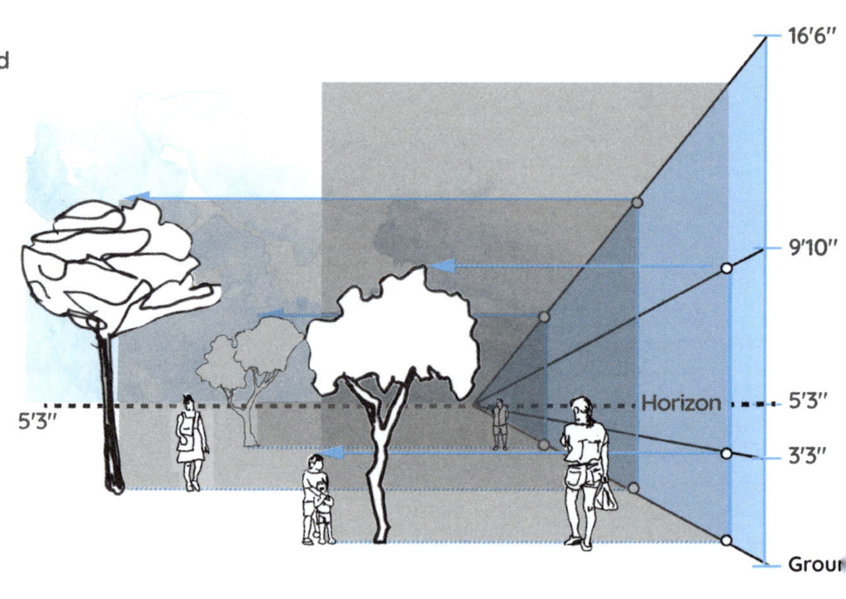

Noting the heights along the edge of the drawing allows us to position them precisely as a function of their depth.

Heights are calculated using a back-and-forth between the ground and an imaginary wall along the edge of the drawing. We will call this operation the "scale of heights."

Width

Since we know all the heights in the drawing, thanks to the measurement of the horizon, we can deduce from that all of the widths along the frontal plane. All we have to do is swivel one of the heights (using a compass, T-square, or ruler) and from that deduce the distance relative to the horizon.

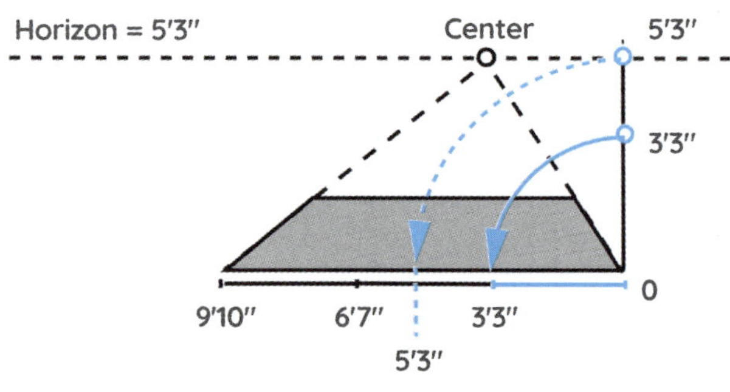

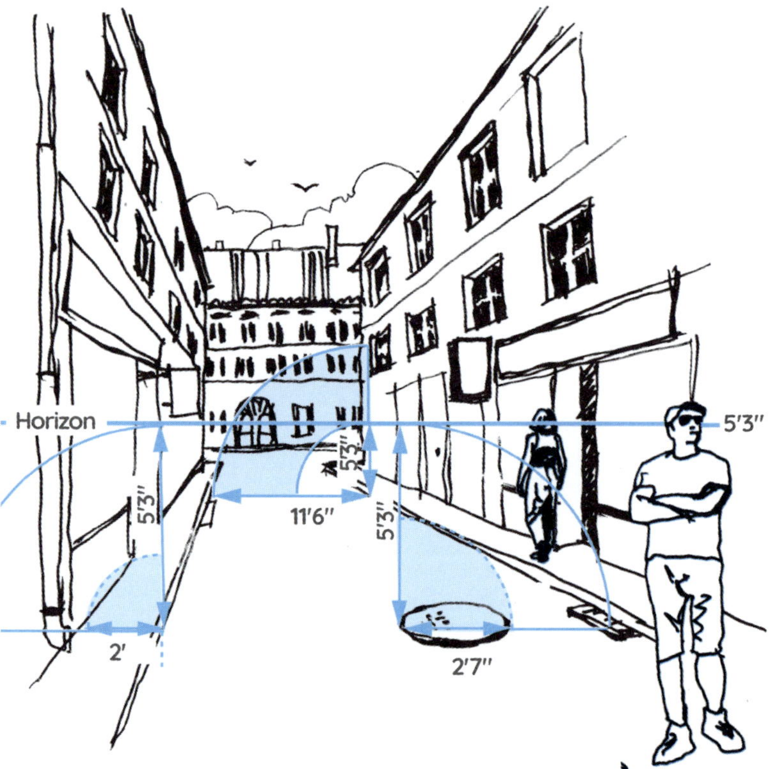

On the right-hand drawing, the horizon is at 5'3". Thus, the street is 11'6" wide, the manhole cover is 2'7" in diameter, and the sidewalk is 2' wide.

Paris, rue de la Corderie

Depth

Knowing how to establish measurements
of height and width on the frontal plane,
we can now deduce depths by using the
intersections at 45°.

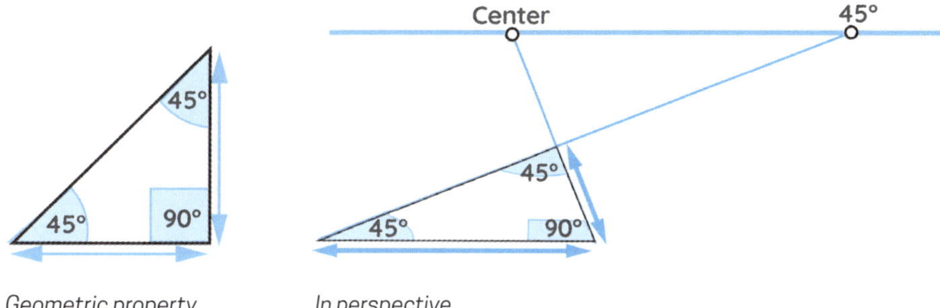

Geometric property   *In perspective*

In this example, two tables, each 3'3" high, 3'3" wide, and 9'10"
long are drawn within a frontal plane.

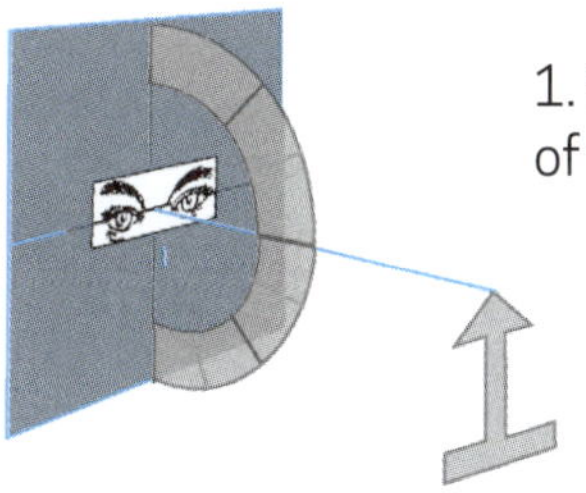

1. Find the widths as a function
of the height of the horizon.

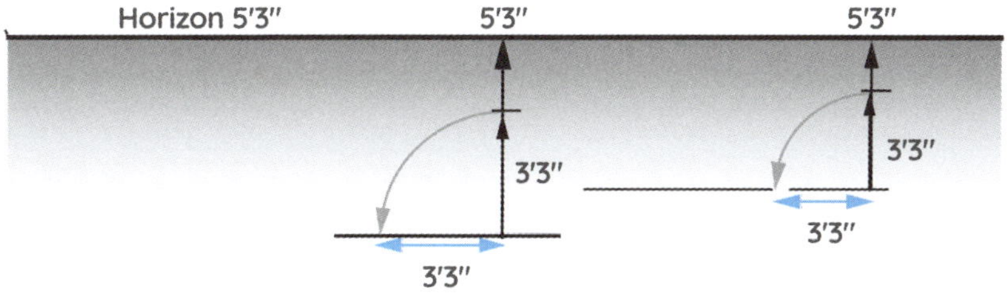

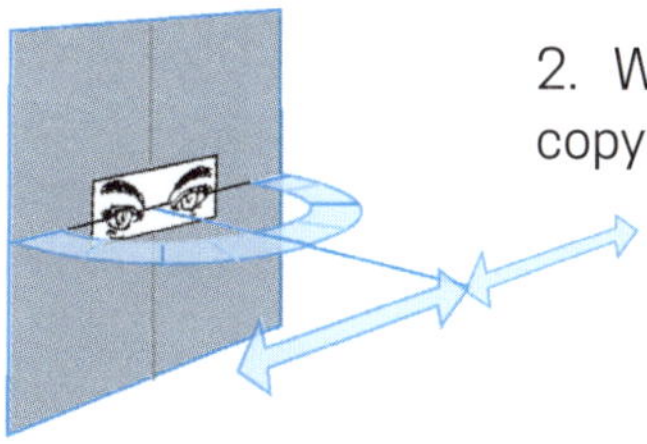

2. Within the frontal plane,
copy the depths to be found.

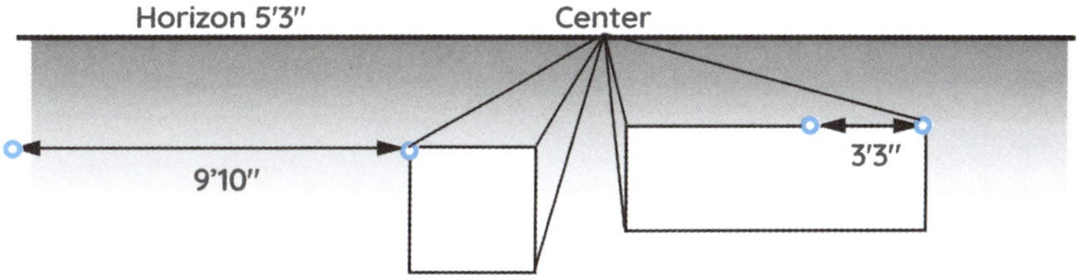

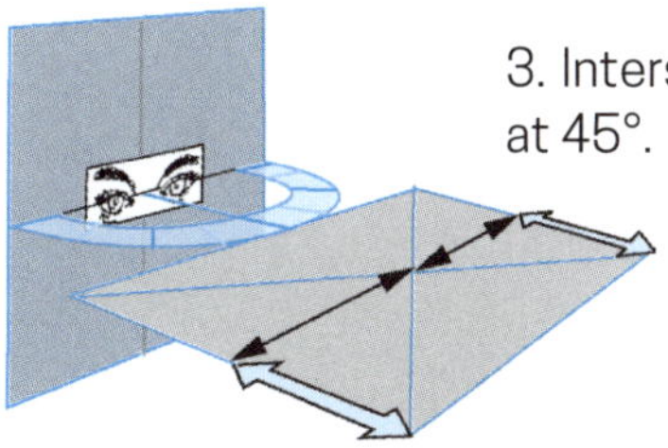

3. Intersect with the direction
at 45°.

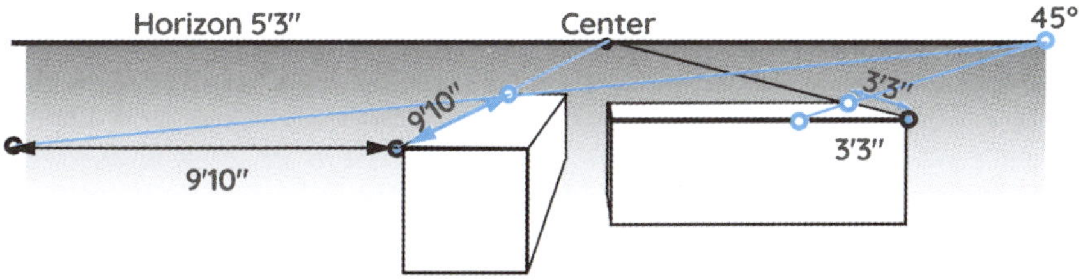

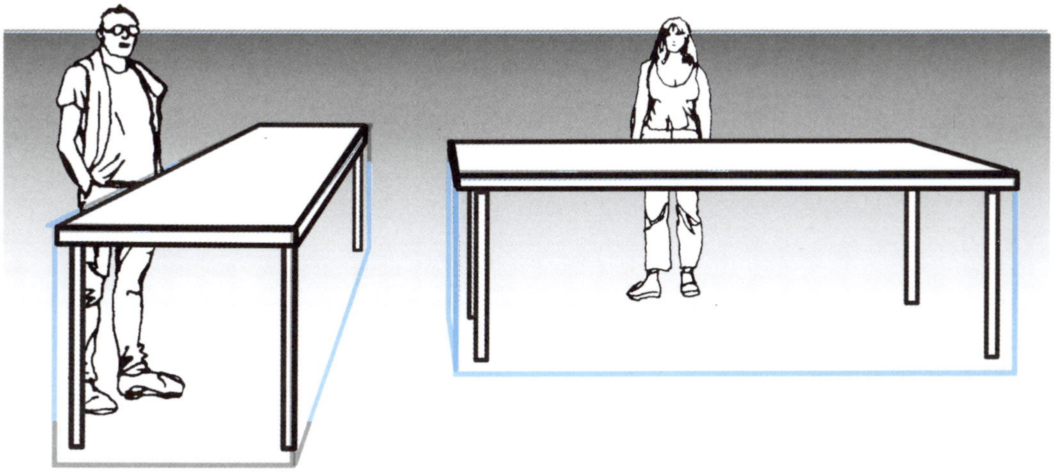

Distances

Starting from the Artist

The artist has to be able to express how far away the objects or architectural elements are that are being represented. Are they far away? Close up? What is the distance exactly? To get a depth scale, we will use the following geometric property: at 45° downward, the artist's gaze hits the ground at a distance H that is equal to the height of the artist's eyes. For example, if Mitsuko is 5'3" tall, her eyes will be 4'11" from the ground (H = 4'11"). If Siegfried is 6'3", his eyes will be 5'11" from the ground (H = 5'11").

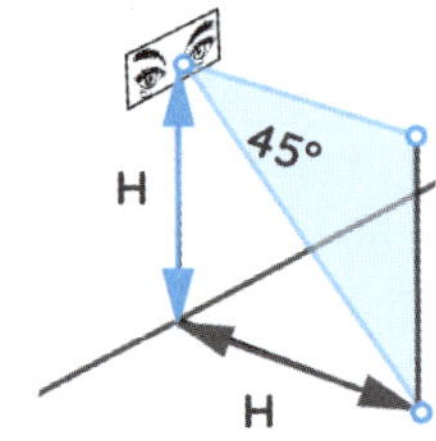

In perspective drawing, this point will be the same distance from the center as a point at 45°.

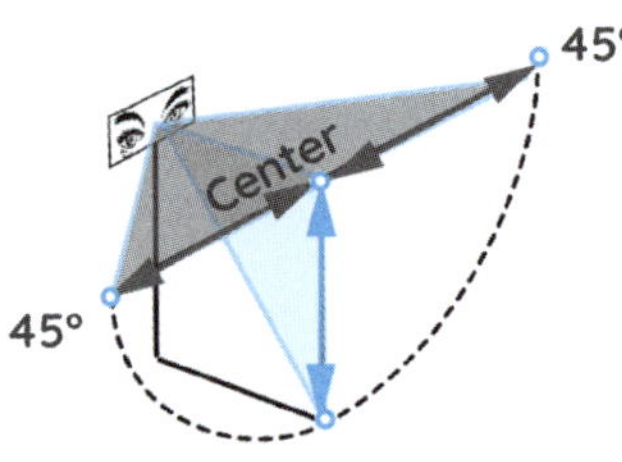

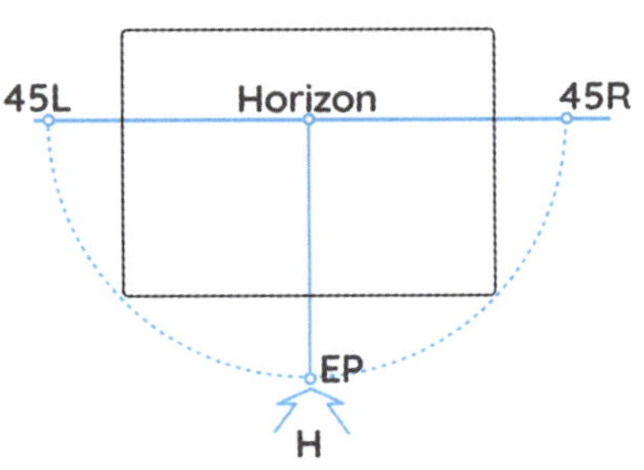

1. The distance from EP (in perspective) to the artist's feet is thus equal to the height of the artist's eyes (H).

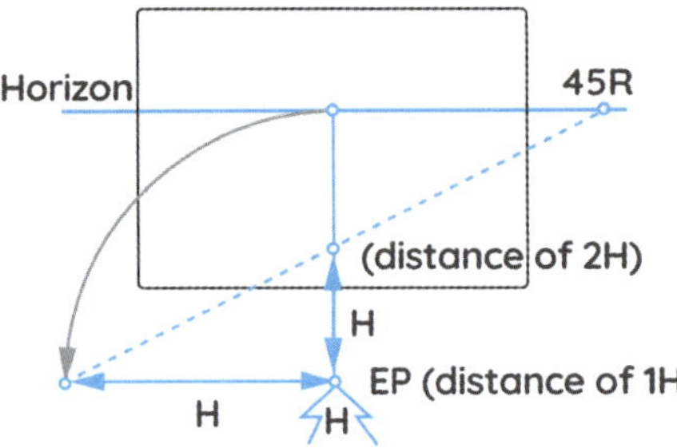

2. The measurement H, copied onto the frontal plane and directed at an angle of 45°, will intersect with the central axis at the same depth (H) (see drawing labeled **In perspective**, p. 19).

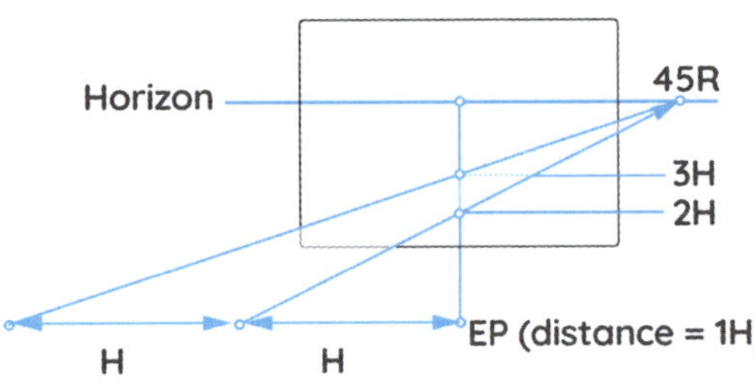

3. We can repeat this operation an infinite number of times (see **Triangulation**, p. 16).

In this way, we obtain a depth scale based on the height of our horizon, which will allow us to construct a template for all our perspectives based on our height.

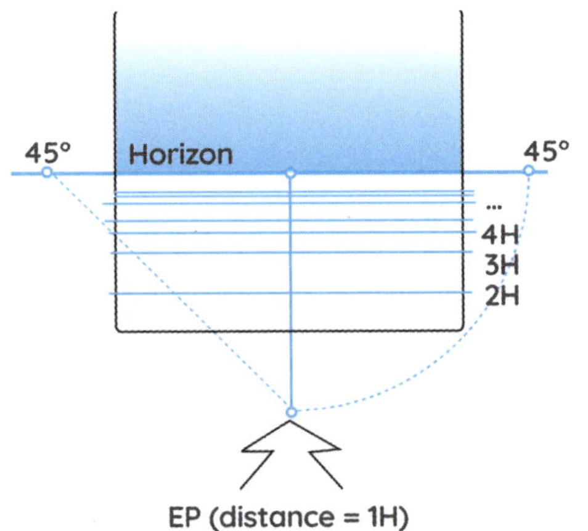

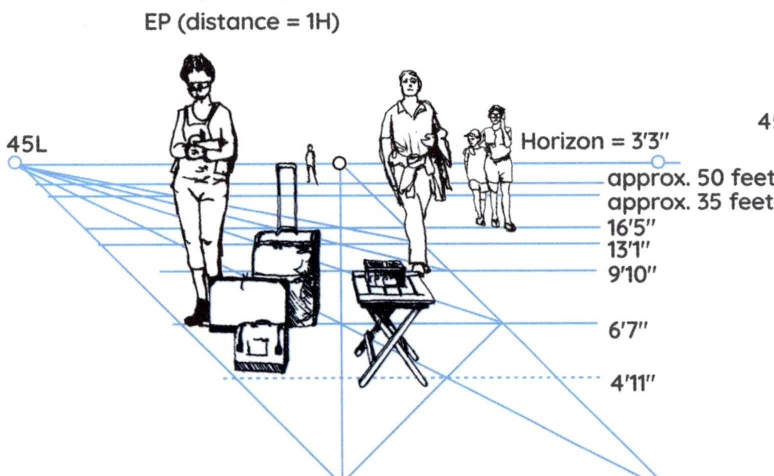

The artist is seated and their eyes are 3'3" above the ground.

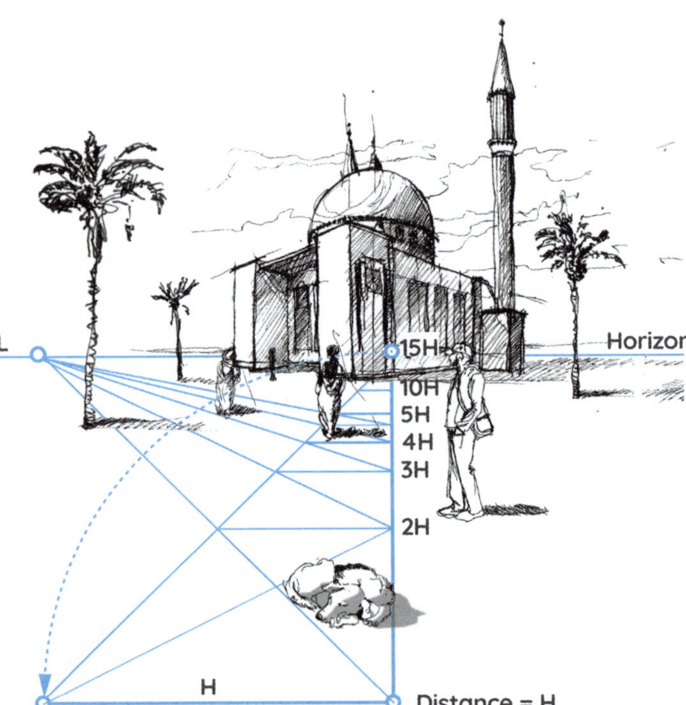

Here, the artist is standing up and their eyes are at height H above the ground.

In a Particular Direction

Now we are in a position to copy a measurement of width, height, and depth, but this does not allow us to establish a distance in a particular direction.

For that, we will use a slope of 45° in the direction we want.

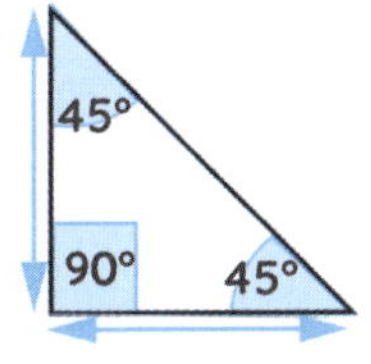

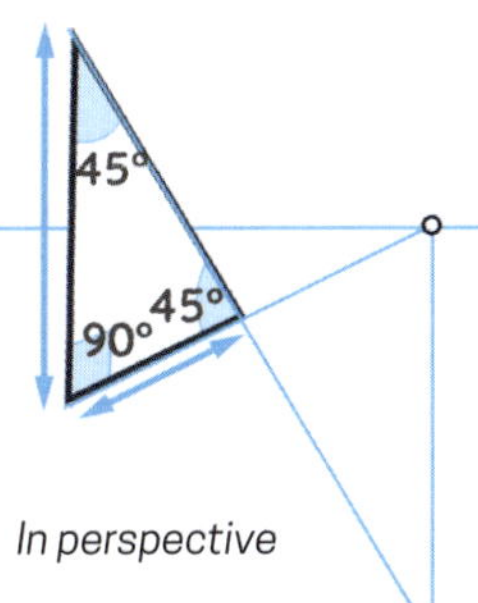

Geometric property

In perspective

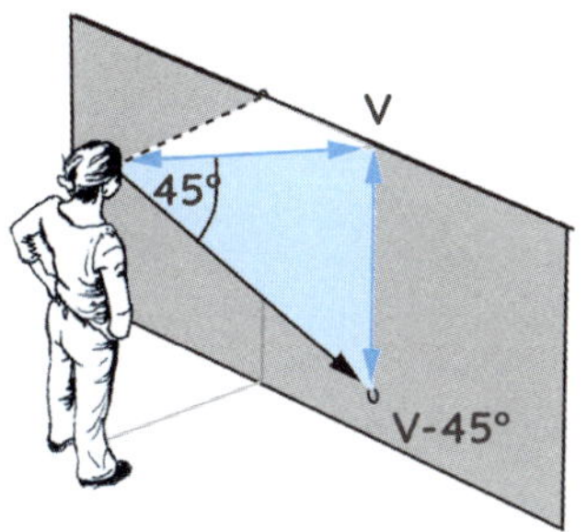

To find the position of the vanishing point at 45° below the chosen direction (V), all we have to do is copy the distance from our eye to the vanishing point underneath point V.

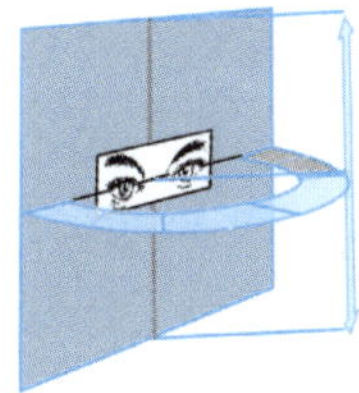

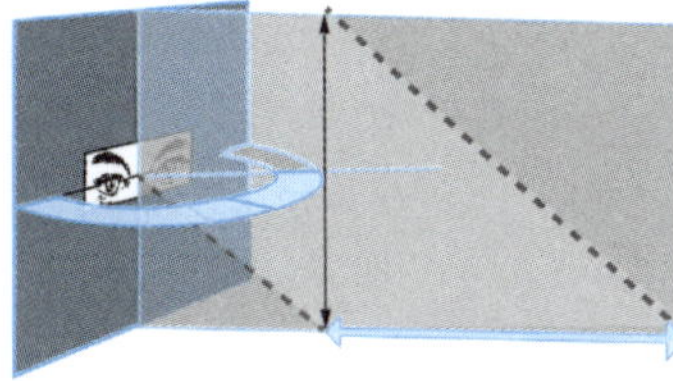

Any height can then be transposed into depth.

Imagine that we want to establish a precise measurement from point A in direction V.

1. We use the frontal plane to measure the direction of the height that we want to transpose toward point V (here, 2H).

2. An intersection at 45° downward will give us the same measurement in the direction of point V.

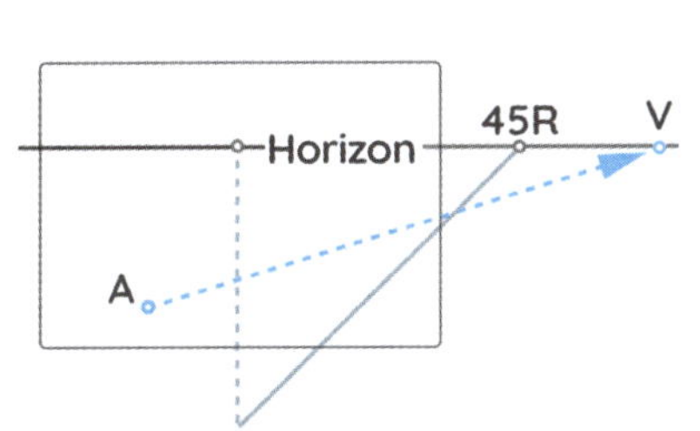

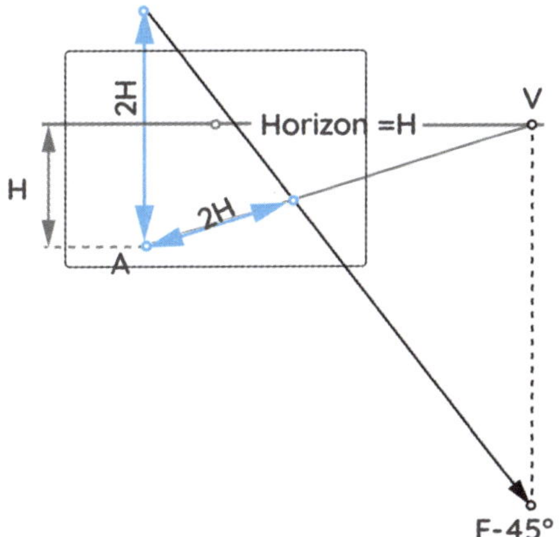

We just use the compass to find a direction 45° below point V.

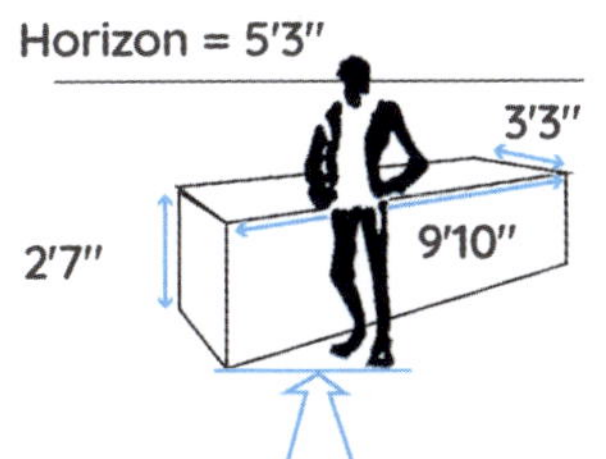

Below, we have put this measurement and distance into practice to draw a table that is 9'10" away from us and that is 2'7" tall, 3'3" wide, and 9'10" long.

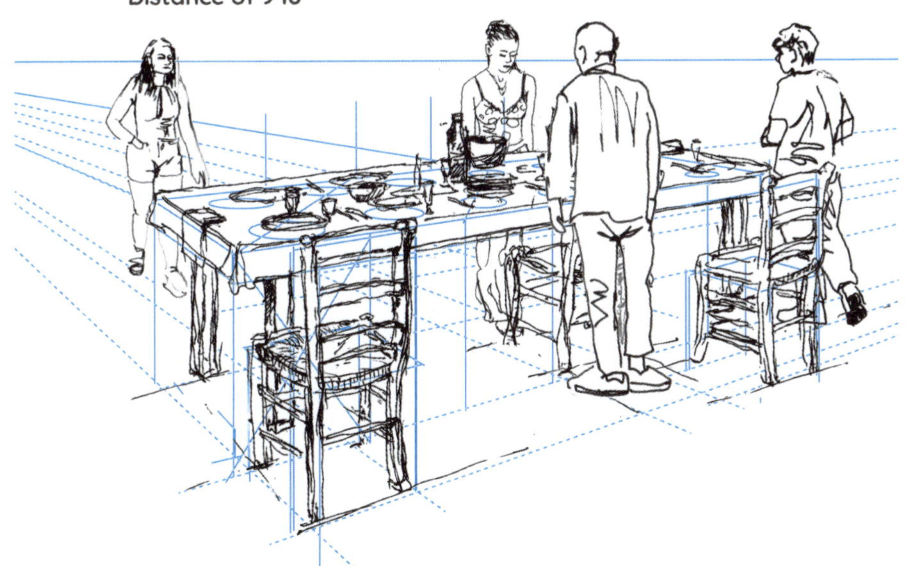

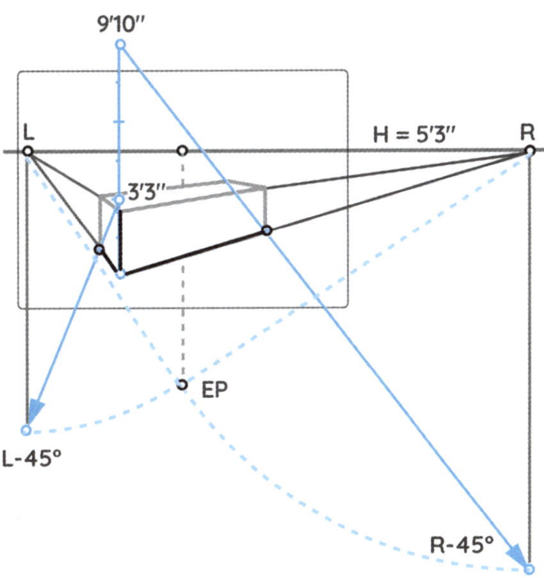

Ellipses

An ellipse is a regular curve that has a major axis and a minor axis (fig. 1). A circle seen in perspective is also an ellipse, which is why it is a good thing to know how to draw an ellipse straight-on from above before trying it in perspective (fig. 2).

Practicing drawing ellipses is a good way to learn and allows you to demonstrate a concrete awareness of the relationship between width and depth in a spatial reconstitution.

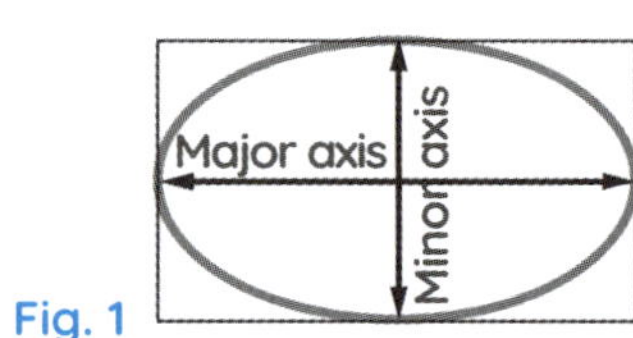

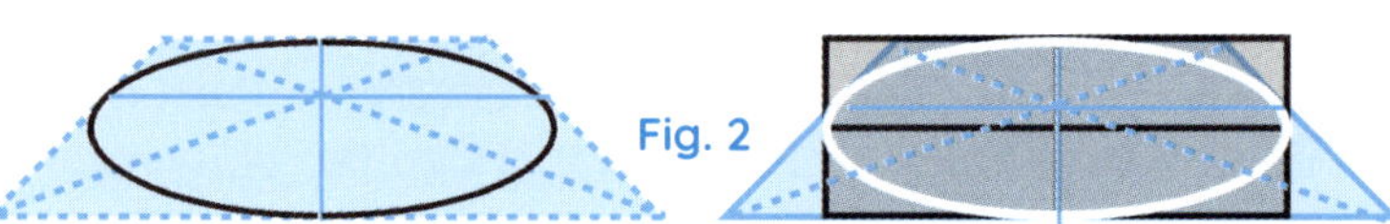

Drawing the View from Above

By shifting the axes

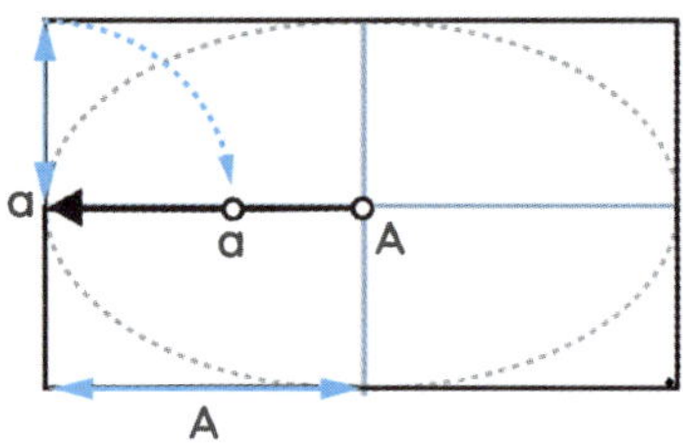
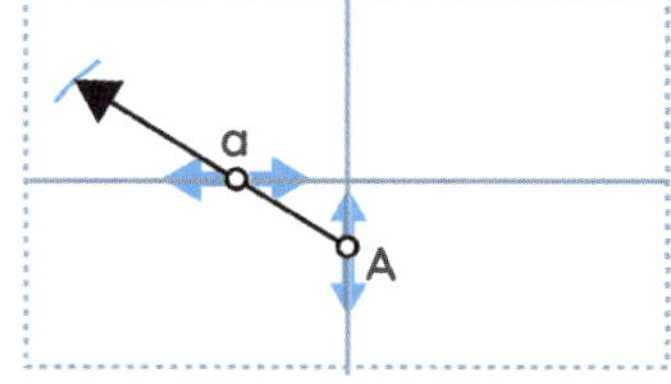
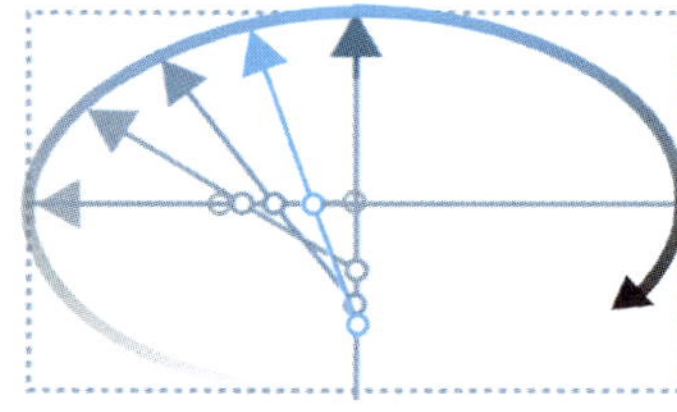
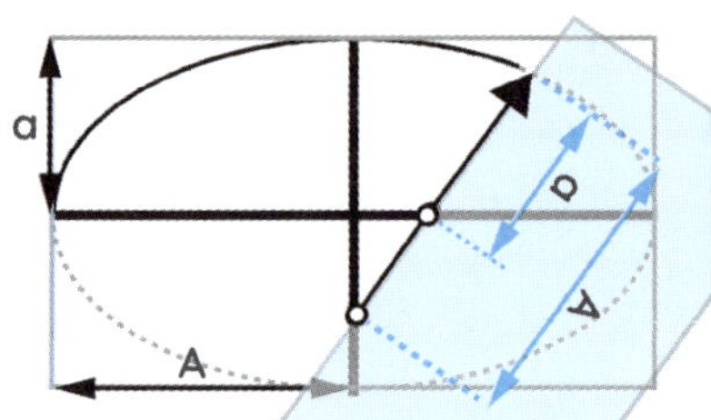

In the rectangle that is going to contain the ellipse, fold down half of the small axis (a) onto half of the major axis (A).

Shift the resulting assembly onto the opposite axes while directing it toward its end: point A shifts onto the minor axis and point a shifts onto the major axis.

The artist can use the edge of a sheet of paper to find the middle of the minor axis and the middle of the major axis.

Through geometric plotting

You can find additional points by connecting the midpoint with the corner and the opposing midpoint with the first quarter (half-corner x half-quarter).

This operation can be repeated for each quarter, from top to bottom and from left to right (in other words, eight times altogether).

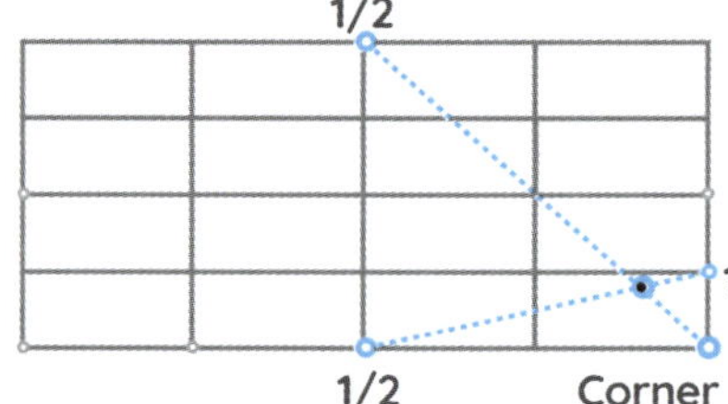

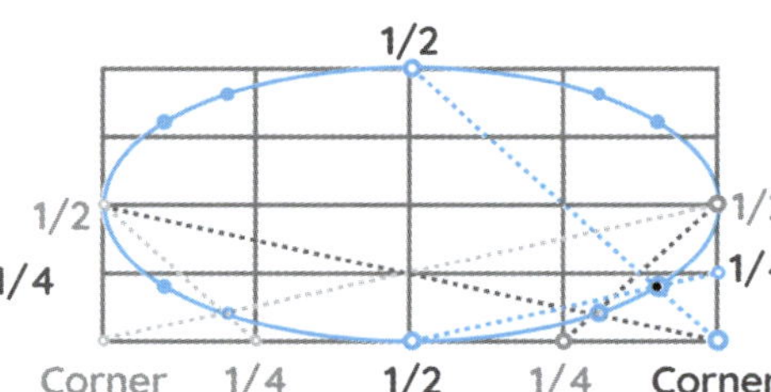

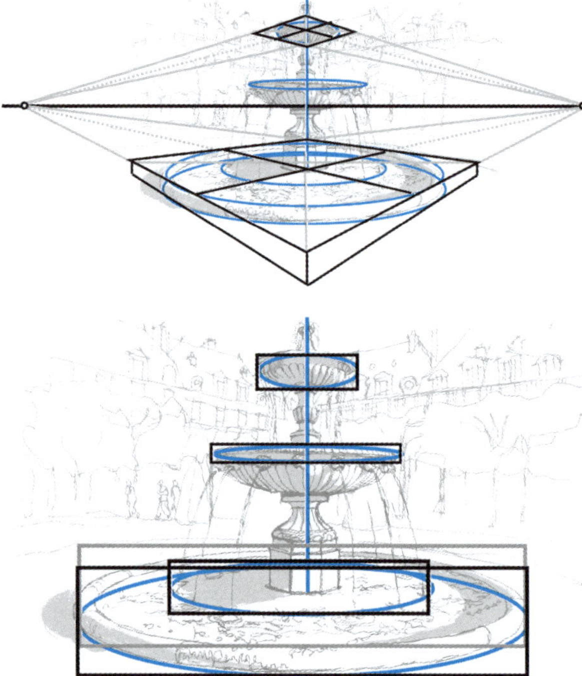

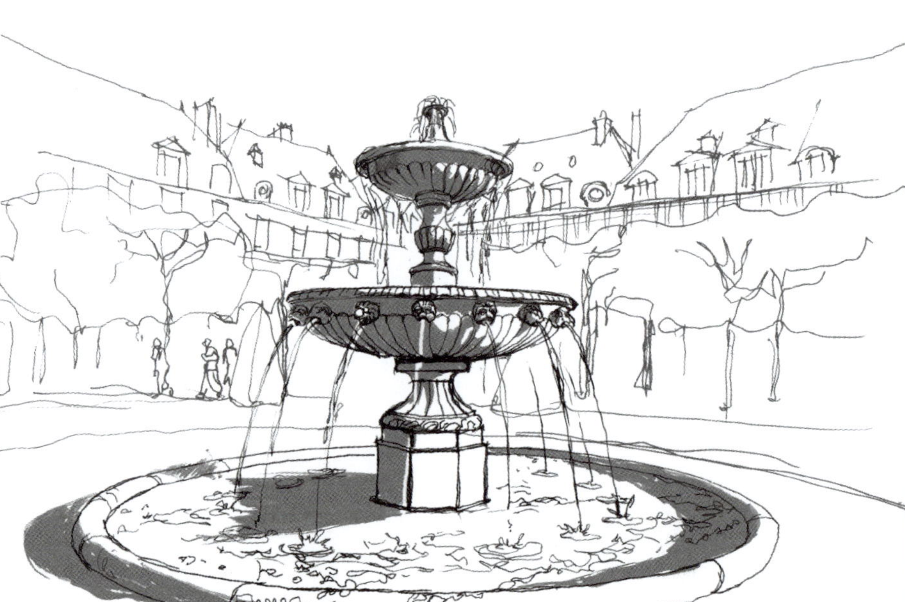

Paris, place des Vosges

Drawing in Perspective

By defining a square that will contain our future ellipse, we already know four points of its outline (the midpoints on each side). But to find the additional intersection points, there are three possible solutions.

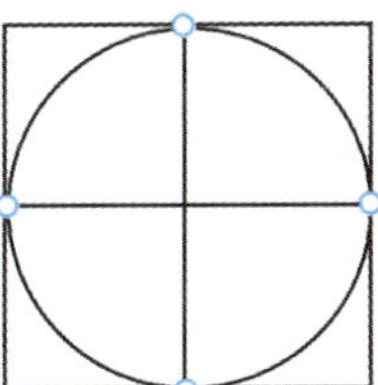

Through geometric plotting

By dividing the sides of the square that will contain the circle into four, we can apply the geometric plotting described above (half-corner x half-quarter).

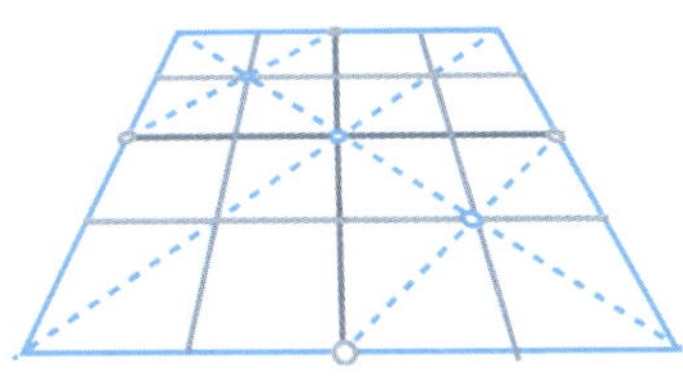

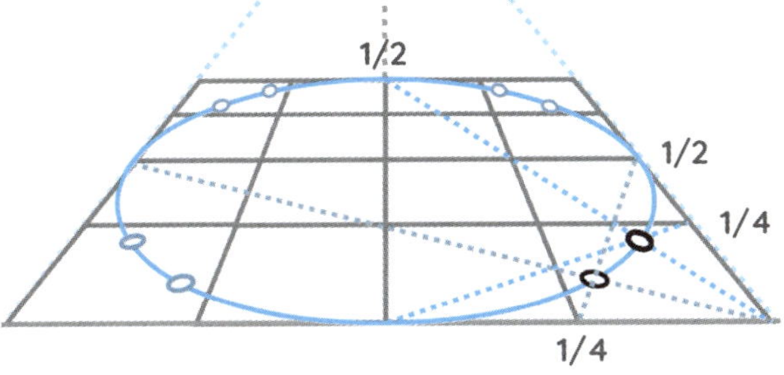

By folding

We can also use a half-circle in the frontal plane to deduce four additional points of intersection along the diagonals.

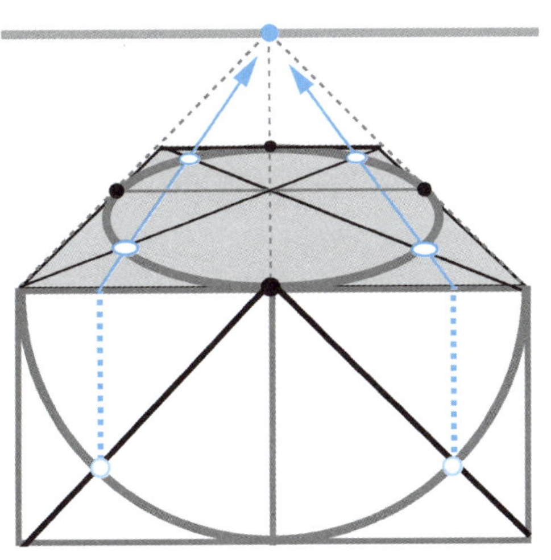

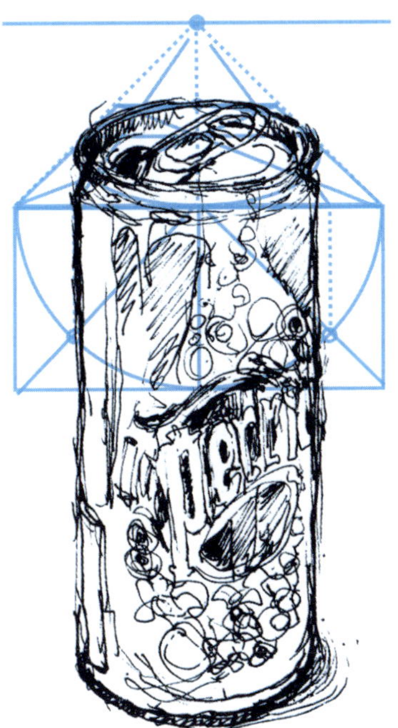

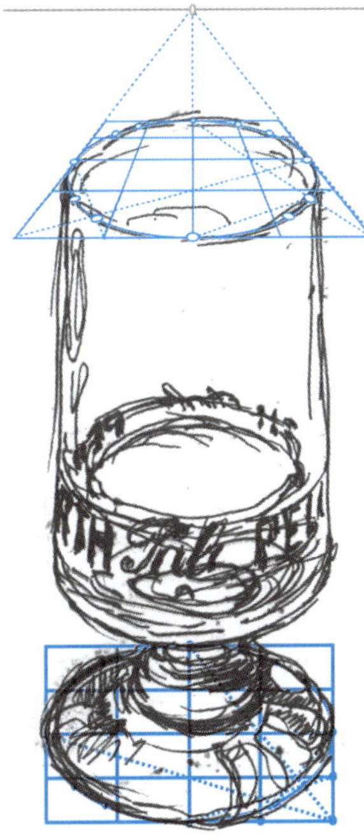

Keep in mind that a circle in perspective is also an ellipse that could have been drawn inside a frontal rectangle.

By shifting the axes

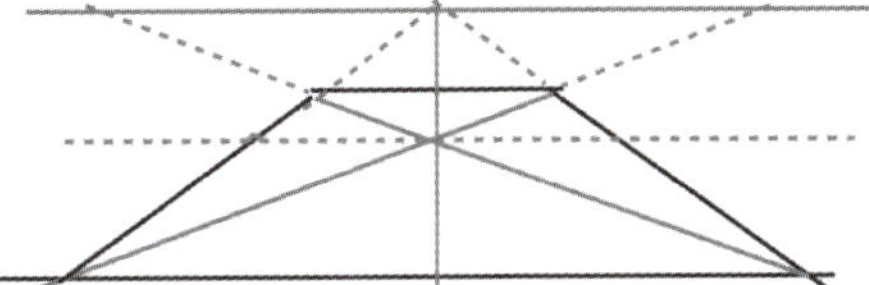

The method of drawing by shifting the axes can be applied directly to a perspective.

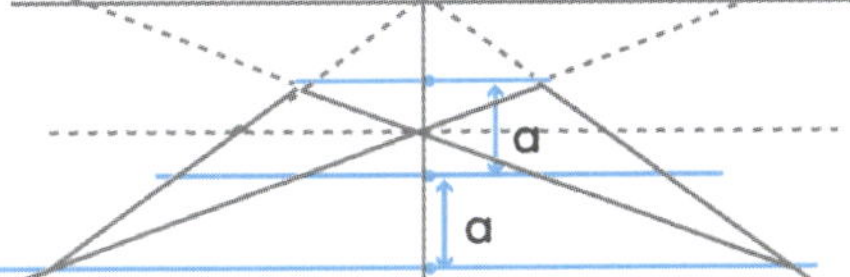

1. Divide the height into two equal parts to obtain half of the minor axis a.

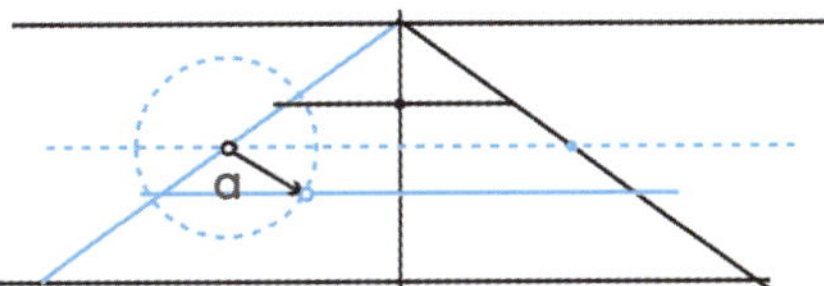

2. Position half of the minor axis between the midpoint of one side in perspective and the major axis of the ellipse.

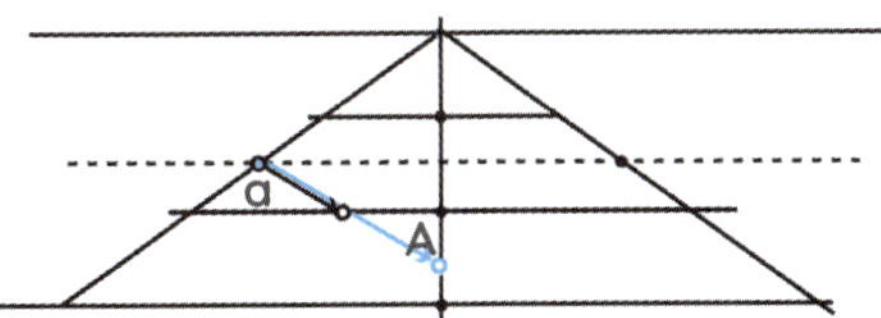

3. Extend the line into the center to obtain the template for the drawing.

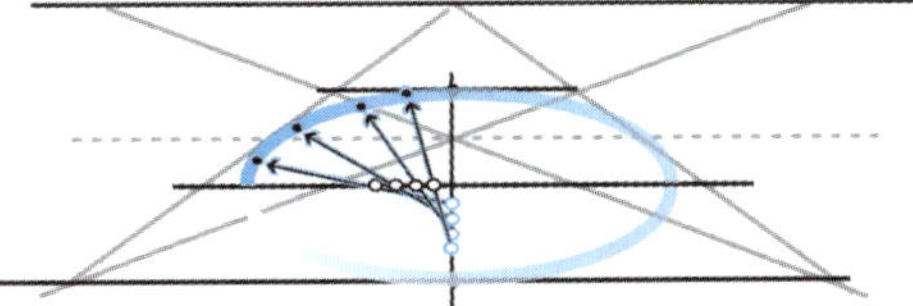

4. Finish the drawing by following this method of shifting.

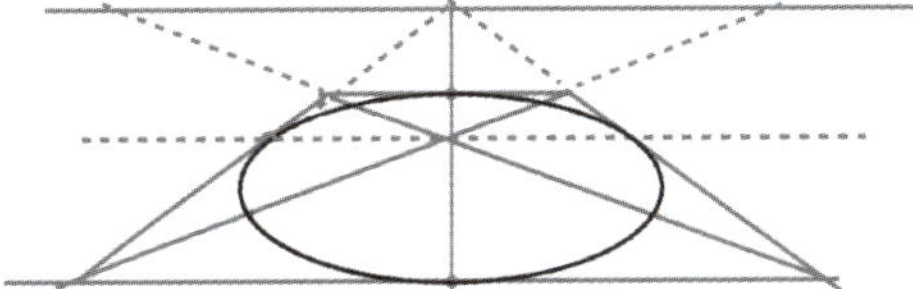

Shadows

Core Shadows and Cast Shadows

Core shadows correspond to the unlighted areas of the shapes that we are working with. Cast shadows are shadows that are projected (or "cast") onto other surfaces, such as the ground.

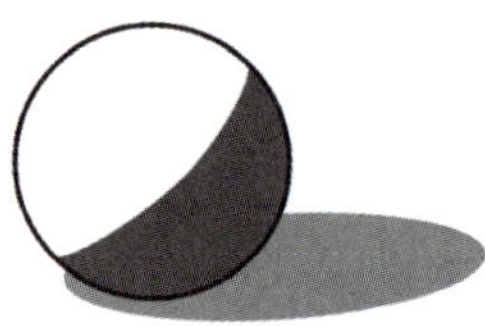

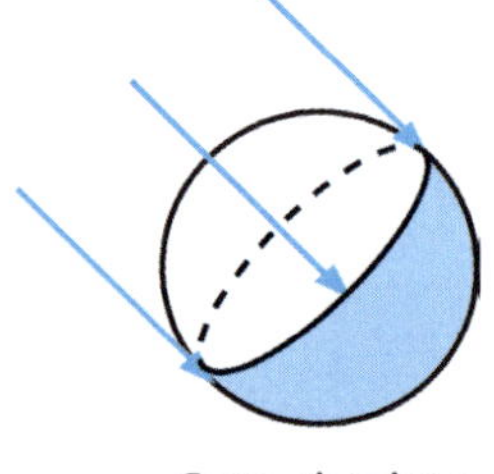

Core shadow

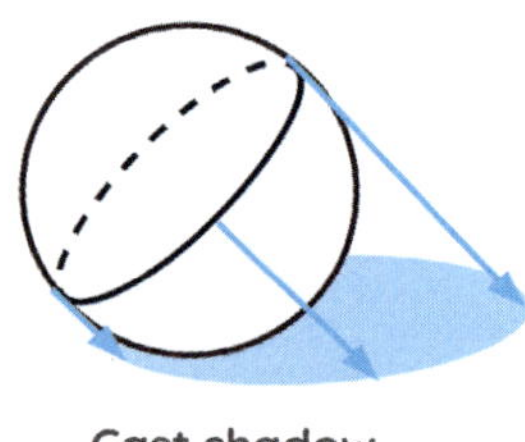

Cast shadow

Direction and Incidence

These two complementary ideas will allow us to find the shadows.

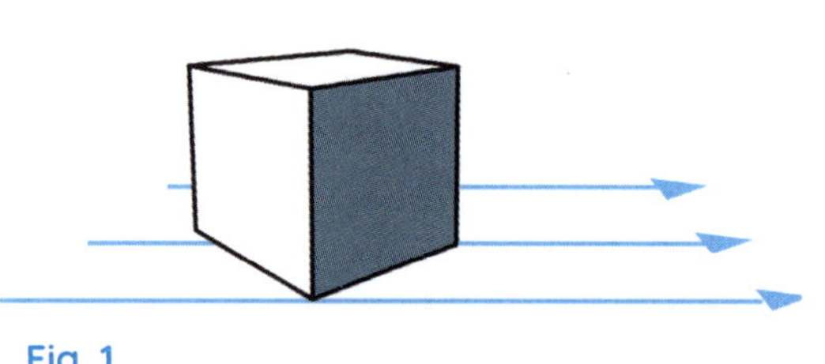

Fig. 1

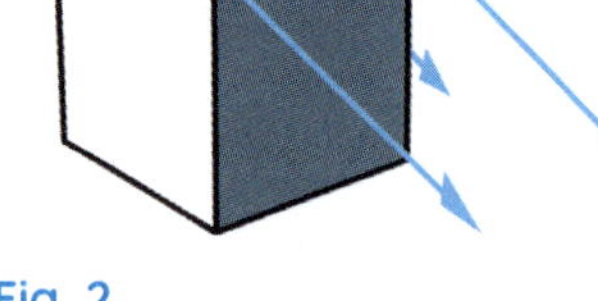

Fig. 2

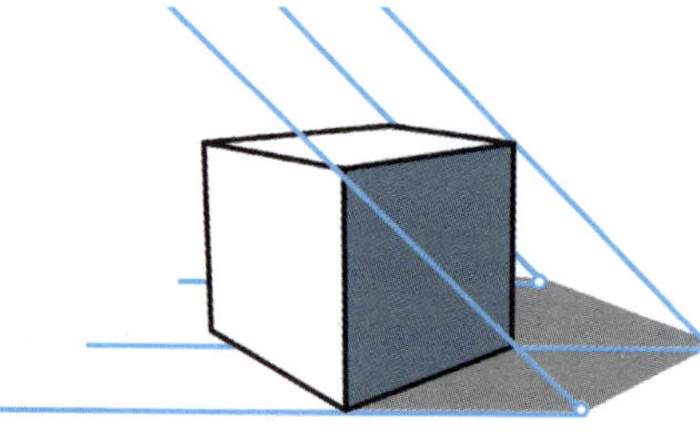

Fig. 3

The **direction** corresponds to the orientation of the lighting on the ground (fig. 1). This is decisive for knowing what surfaces are lit up and for deducing from that where the core shadows will be.

Incidence is the slope at which the rays hit the ground (fig. 2). For every edge of an object, the edge of the shadow will be at the intersection of the direction and the incidence.

The Different Kinds of Lighting

Frontal sun: When the sun is entirely to either our left or our right, it is within the frontal plane. The directions will then all be horizontal and the slopes will all be parallel to each other (with the sun at infinity).

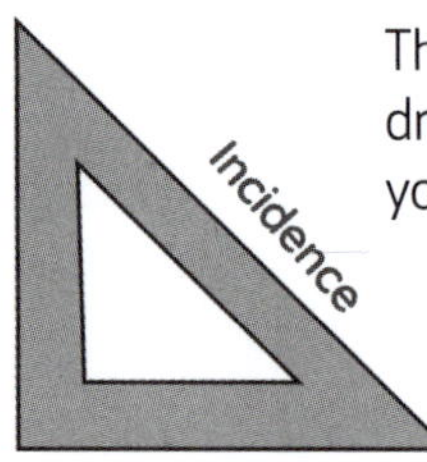

The incidence can be drawn using a triangle or drawing square, according to the angle that you want to give to the lighting.

Advantages and Disadvantages:

- the shadows will be easier to draw, and keeping an equal balance of shadows and light will provide more contrast;
- be careful, though, because lengthening the drawing toward the side of the shadows could produce distortions.

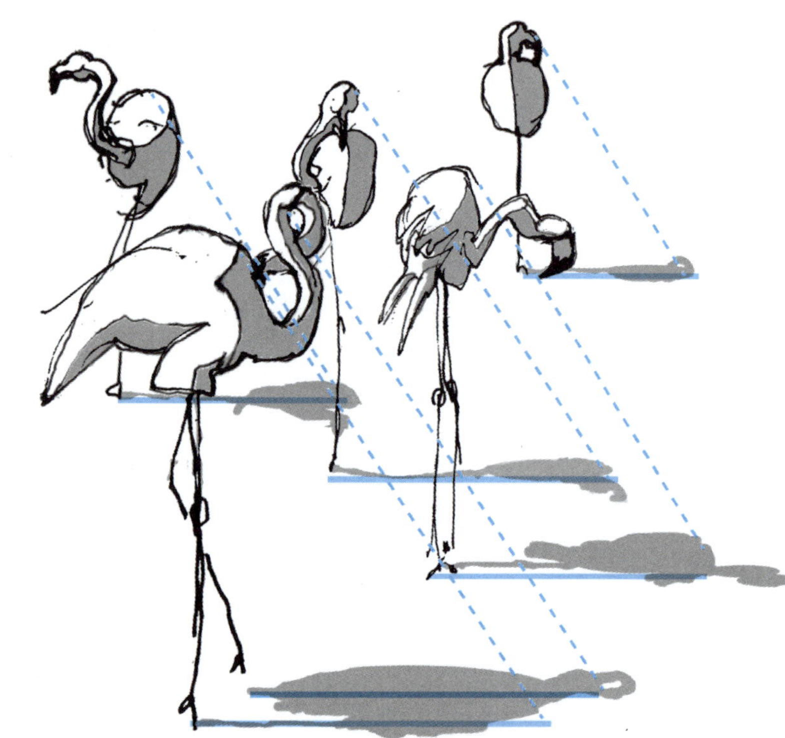

Backlighting: The sun is facing the artist and is potentially visible in the drawing area. The lighting will be considered as a rising slope (see **Slopes**, p. 14).

Sun behind you: The sun is behind the artist. In this case, the lighting will be considered as a descending slope (see **Slopes**, p. 14).

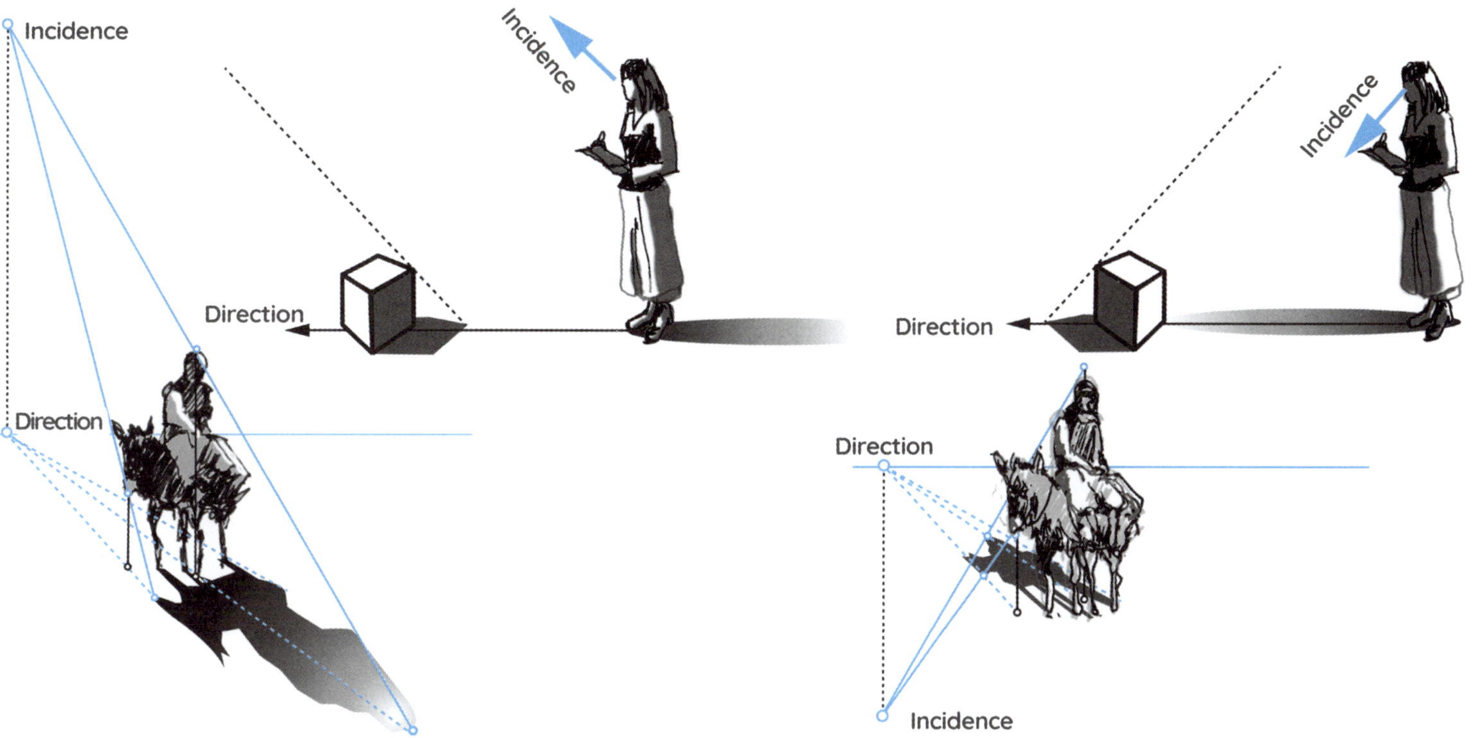

The direction is on the horizon. The incidence is above the horizon (the sun itself.)

The direction is on the horizon. The incidence is below the horizon (diametrically opposed to the sun).

Advantages and disadvantages:

- the shadows are very visible;
- be careful because the subject is poorly lit (with backlighting) and you can expect distortions in front of the scene.

Advantages and disadvantages:

- the scene is well lit;
- be careful because the shadows will be small and they will be partially masked by the subject.

Spot lighting: This could be in an interior scene, in the context of urban lighting, or on a stage set. The lighting will have to be spatially localized.

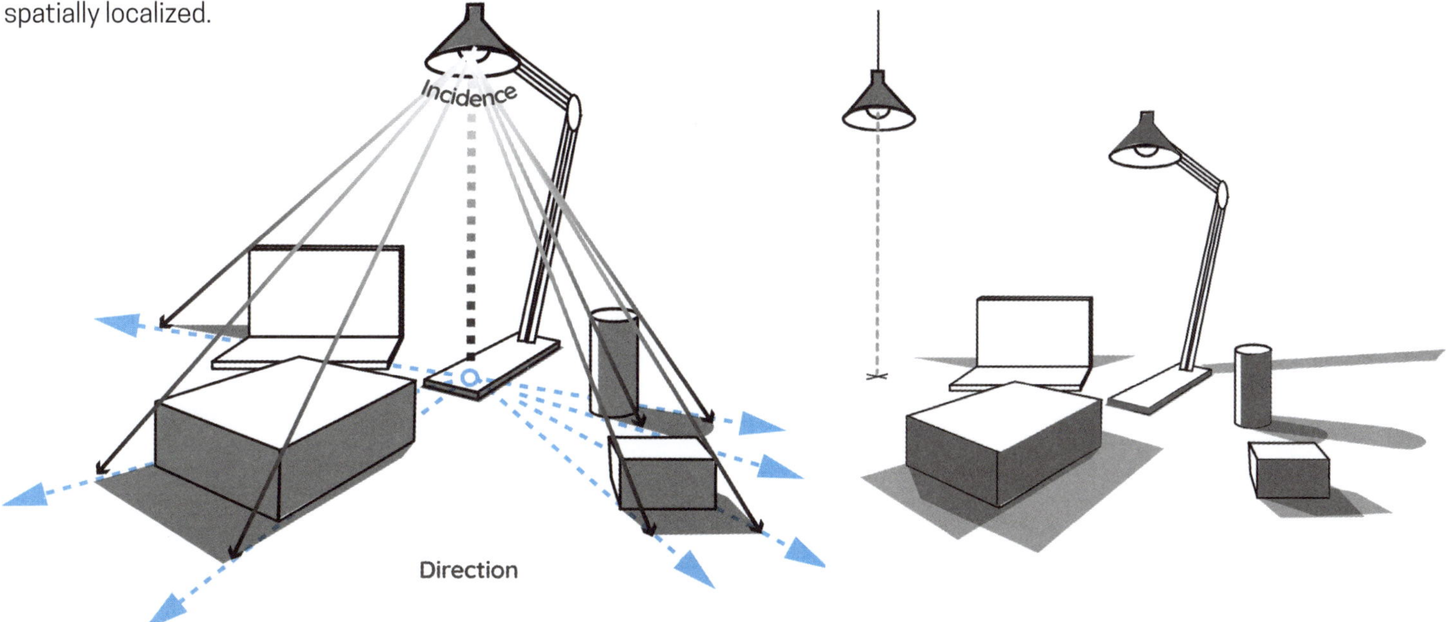

The direction is on the ground (straight down from the light source). The incidence is the light source itself.

When there are multiple light sources, the lights are additive.

Reflections

On a Horizontal Surface

We must consider a reflection as a world glued upside-down underneath the reflective surface (fig. 1). The heights are duplicated, just as they are (not shortened), with respect to their distance from the reflecting surface. The vanishing points of the real world remain valid for the reflections (fig. 2). If the reflecting area is not in contact with the scene, the reflection must be drawn to cover all of the surface of the ground (fig. 3), and then the nonreflective areas can be eliminated (fig. 4).

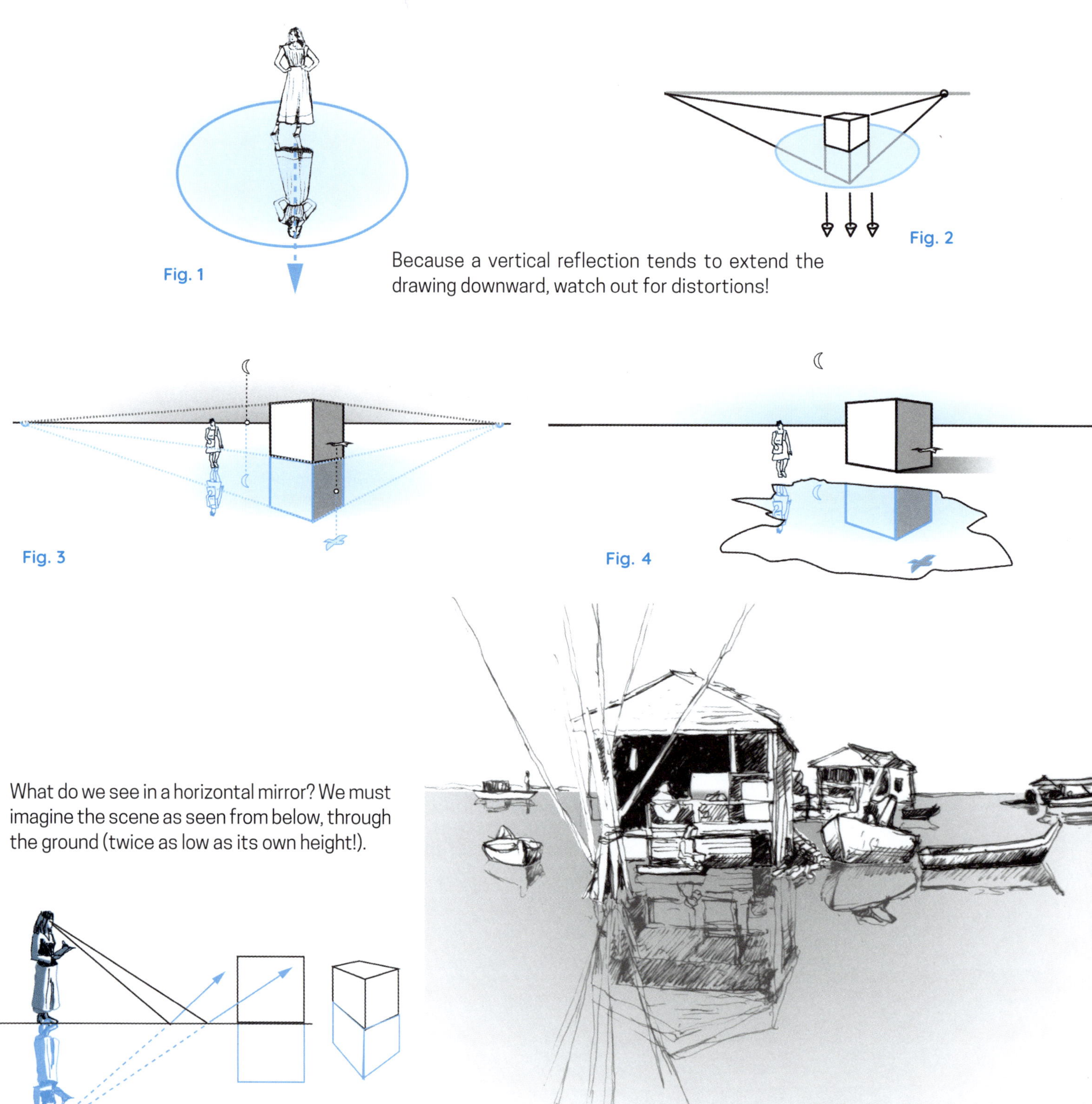

Fig. 1

Fig. 2

Because a vertical reflection tends to extend the drawing downward, watch out for distortions!

Fig. 3

Fig. 4

What do we see in a horizontal mirror? We must imagine the scene as seen from below, through the ground (twice as low as its own height!).

Cambodia, on Tonlé Sap Lake

On a Vertical Surface

On the surface of a mirror, things are reflected perpendicularly. Thus, if we know the direction of the mirror, we can deduce the direction of its reflection starting from point EP.

What do we see in a vertical mirror? We must imagine the scene as seen by our own reflection, through the mirror (from twice as far away, in the axis of reflection!). Note that compared to the horizon, our reflection is twice as small as the mirror since it is twice as far away.

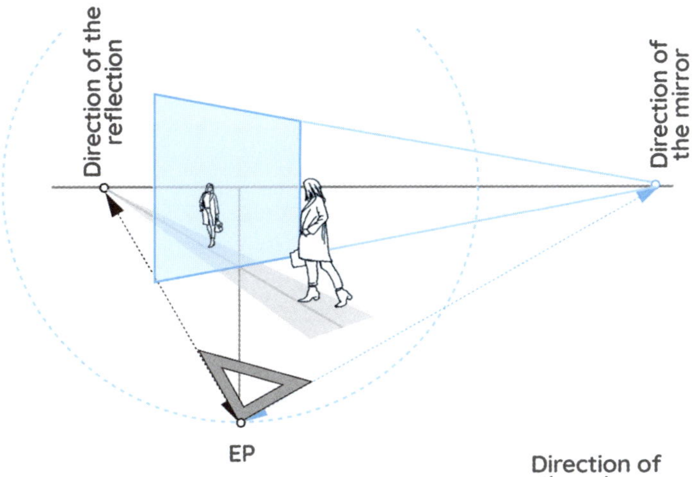

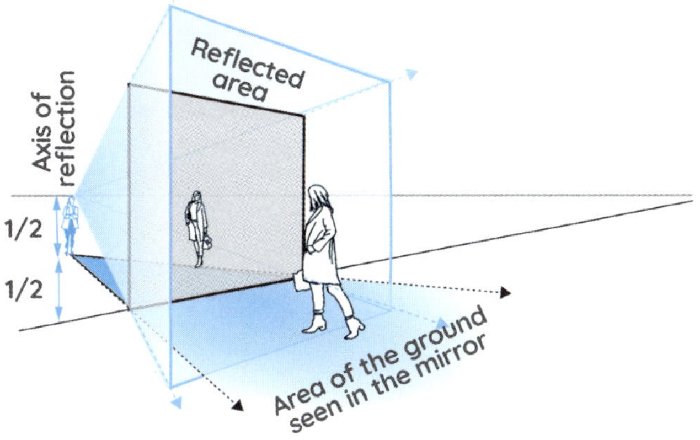

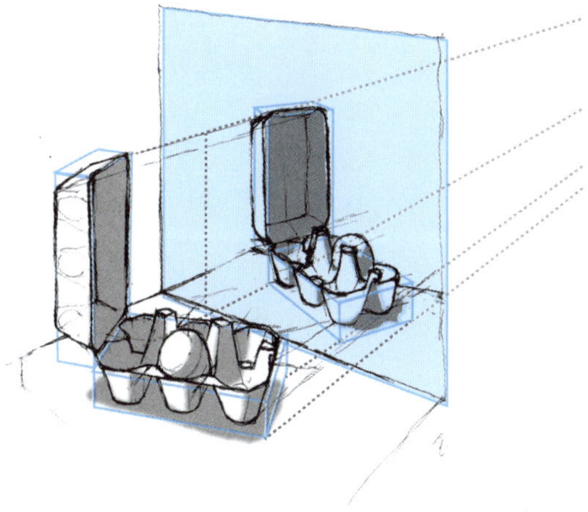

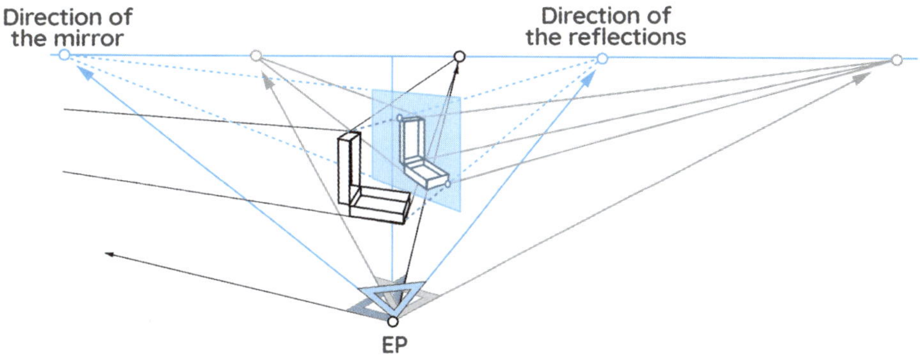

The distance from the object to the mirror is the same as the distance from the mirror to the reflection. It needs to be transposed onto the axis of reflection, taking into account the shortening caused by perspective. If this distance is transposed to the ground, it allows us to find the base of the reflected object.

Transposing Distances: Three Solutions

Geometric, by dividing the height into two equal parts (fig. 1).
Frontal, by transposing a distance onto the frontal plane (fig. 2).
Slope, by finding a direction underneath the axis of reflection (fig. 3).

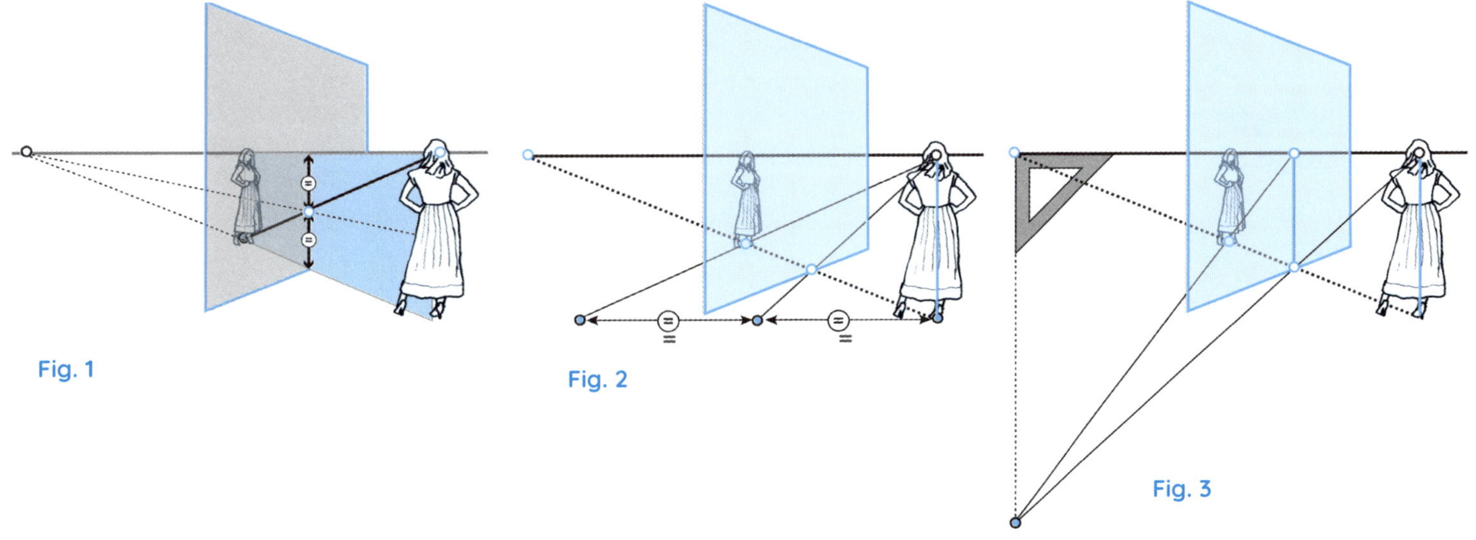

3D Perspective

Upward and Downward

If we look upward or downward, the vertical lines will eventually cross our visual field and we will have to take their direction into account. This will thus be either a perspective from below or a bird's-eye view, which will result in a vanishing point for the vertical lines.

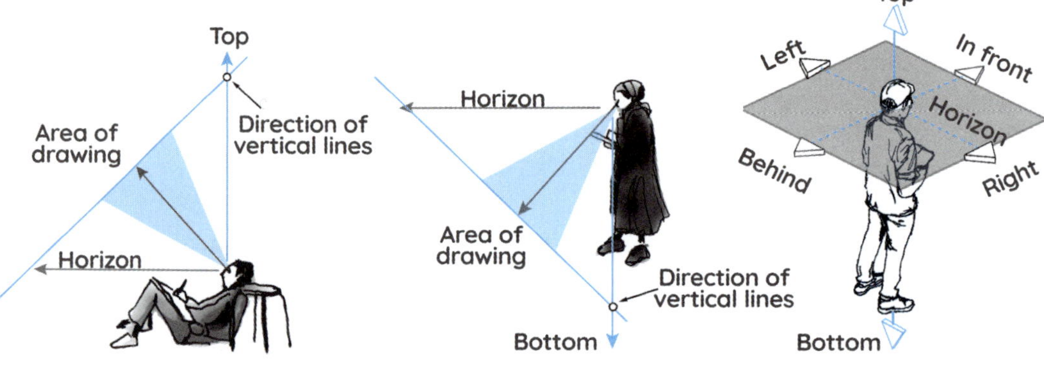

Perspective from below: The vertical lines have a vanishing point toward the top.

Bird's-eye view: The vertical lines have a vanishing point toward the bottom.

We are now entering into a three-dimensional world (front and back, top and bottom, left and right).

Positioning the Vanishing Points through a Diagram of the Scene

We must analyze the visual situation of the artist using a diagram in profile. Where are the artist's eyes, their horizontality, their verticality, and the center of what they are looking at?

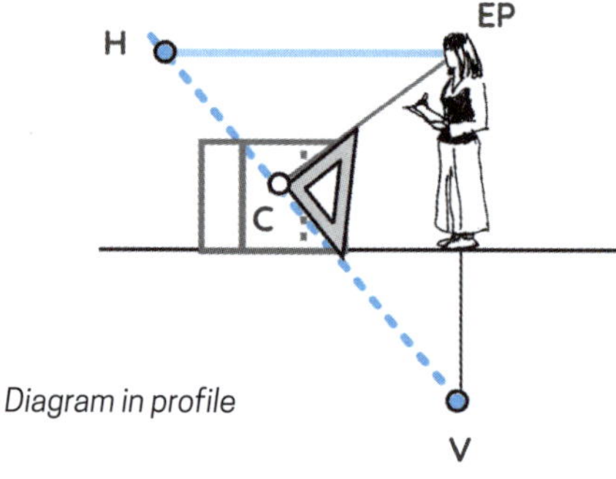

Diagram in profile

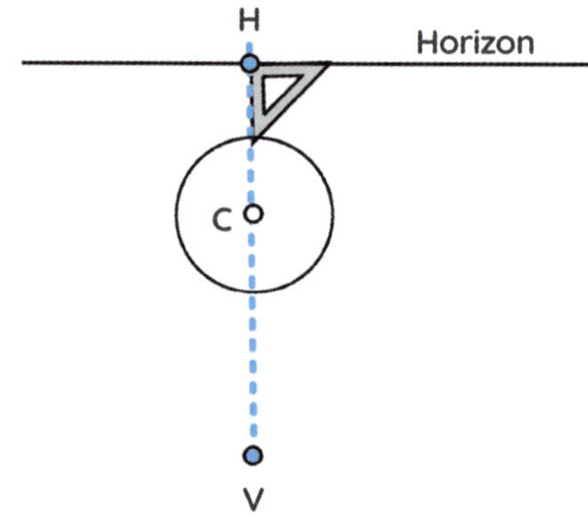

1. Find the position of the eye (EP), the horizon (H), the verticality (V), and the center of the gaze (C).

2. Copy the distance HV (see the diagram in profile on the left) passing through the center of the drawing to position the horizon and the vanishing point of the vertical lines (V).

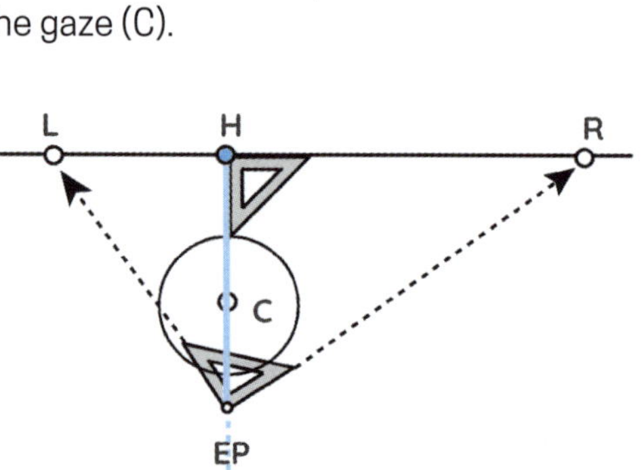

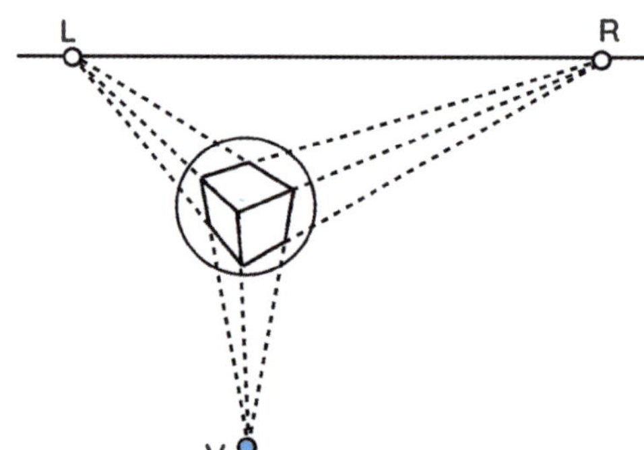

3. Copy the distance EP–H (see the diagram in profile) perpendicular to the horizon and passing through the center of the drawing to choose a right-angle relation to the horizon (L and R).

L — Horizon — R

Bird's-eye view

Greece, Island of Chios

Vertical lines

Positioning the Vanishing Points Using the Visual Field

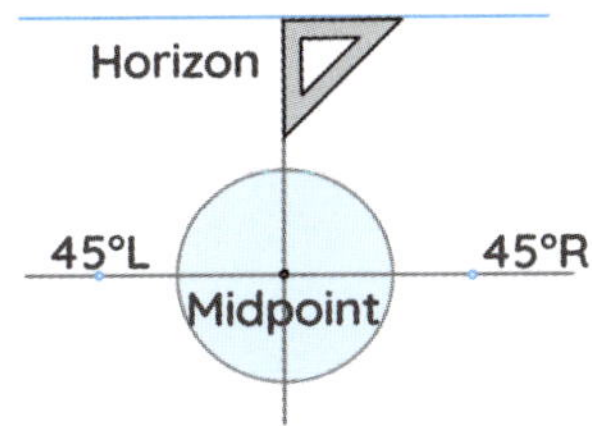

1. Locate the horizon in relation to the visual field.

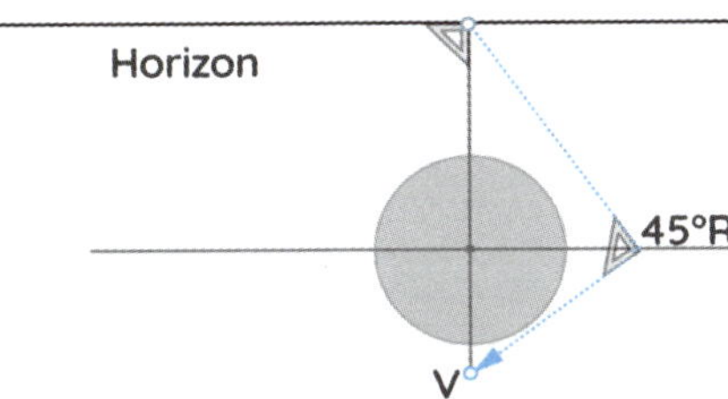

2. Starting at 45°R, the horizontal and the vertical form a right angle. Knowing where the horizon is in front of you (H), you can thus set the vanishing point of the verticals (V).

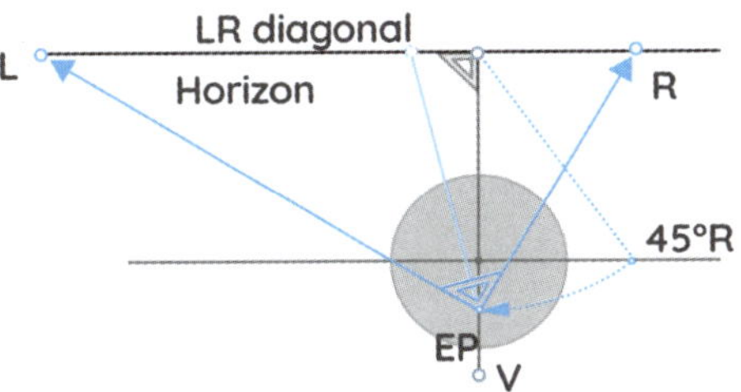

3. By copying the distance H–45°R onto the vertical axis HV, you can position EP and thus define horizontal directions of your choice making a right angle (L and R) (see **Constructing Right Angles**, p. 13).

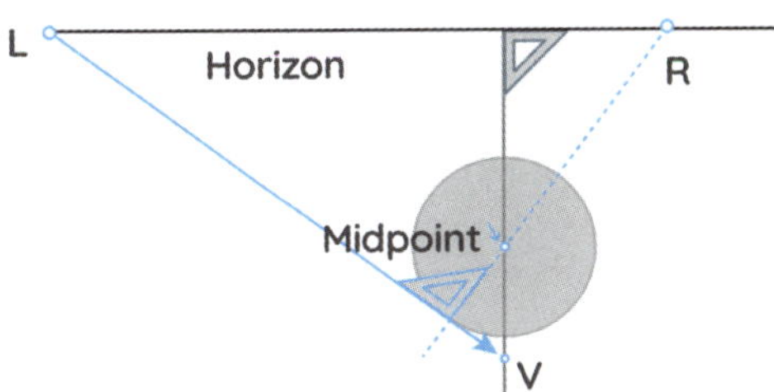

Note that a straight line passing through the midpoint and one of the three vanishing points (L, R, or V) must always be perpendicular to the opposite side.

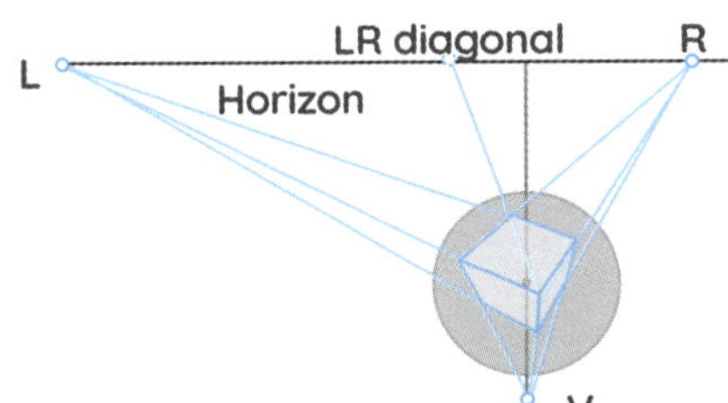

Constructing a cube using the horizontal diagonal: The closer the area of the drawing is to the horizon, the further away the vanishing point of the vertical lines will become.

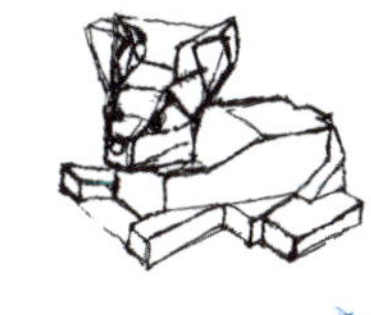

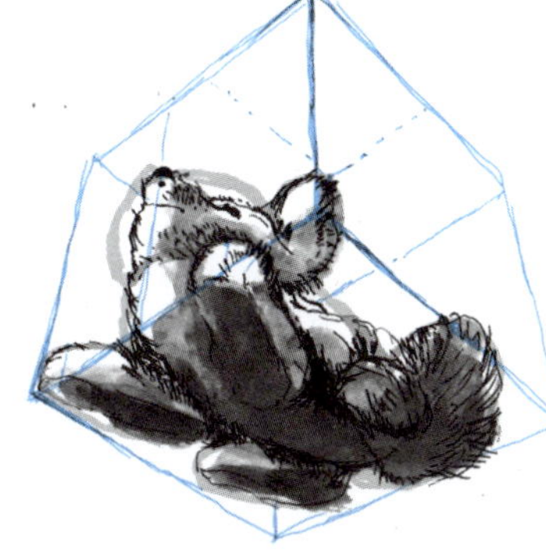

Perspective from below

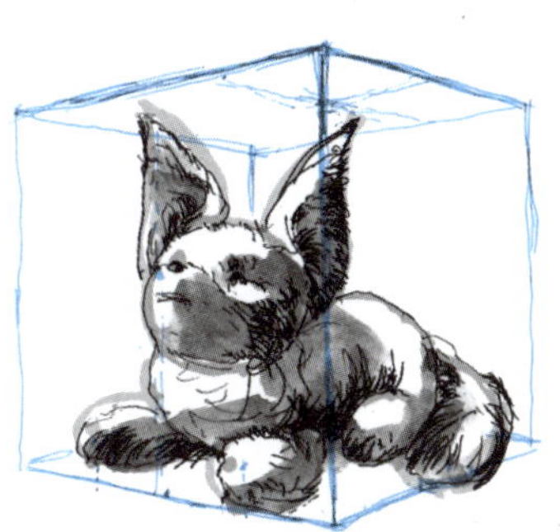

Horizontal perspective

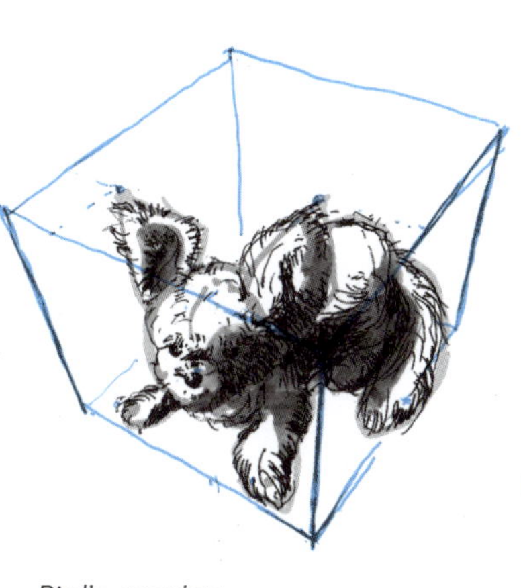

Bird's-eye view

A perspective with three vanishing points will remain correct no matter how you look at it, as long as the horizon is horizontal and the vertical axis goes through the center of the drawing.

Below, all the lines are identical, but oriented differently to maintain a horizontal plane and a vertical axis. Only the shadows have been modified to give the illusion of a different point of view.

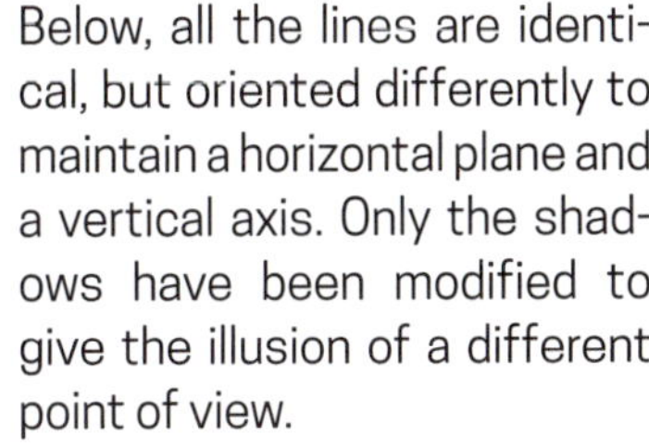

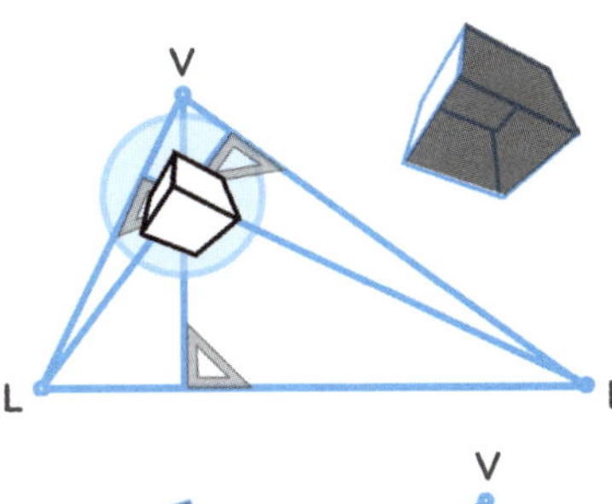

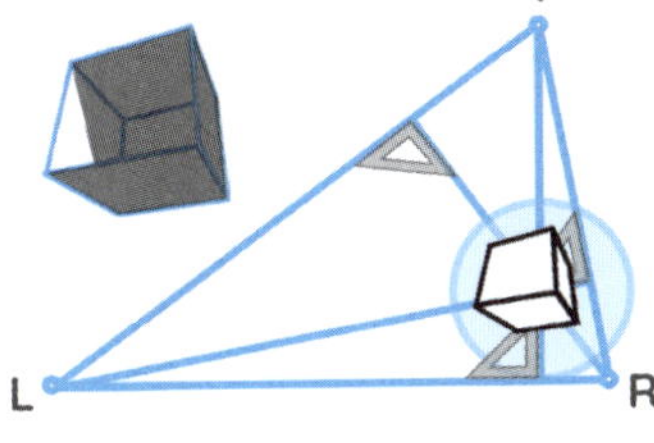

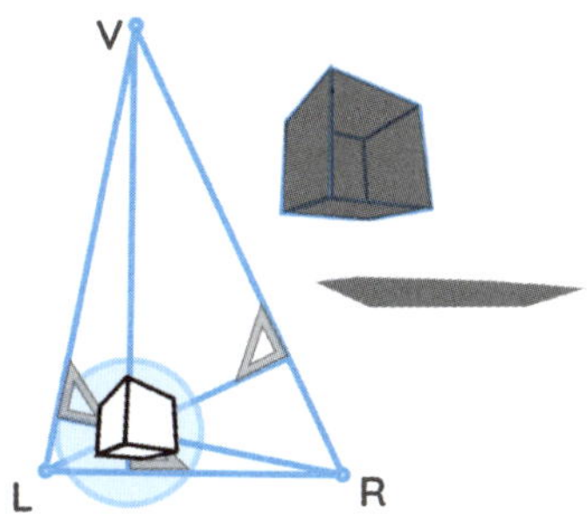

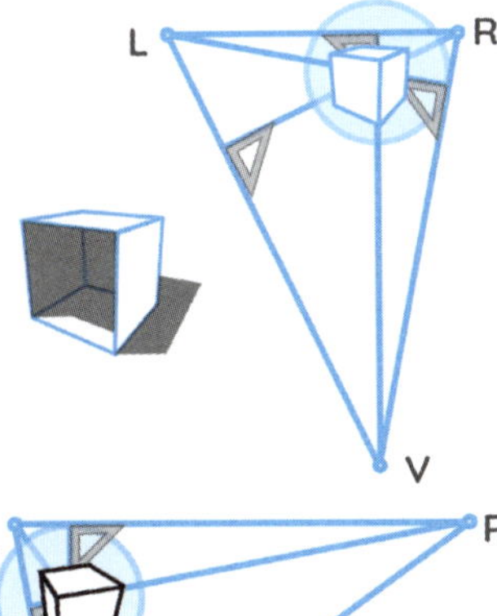

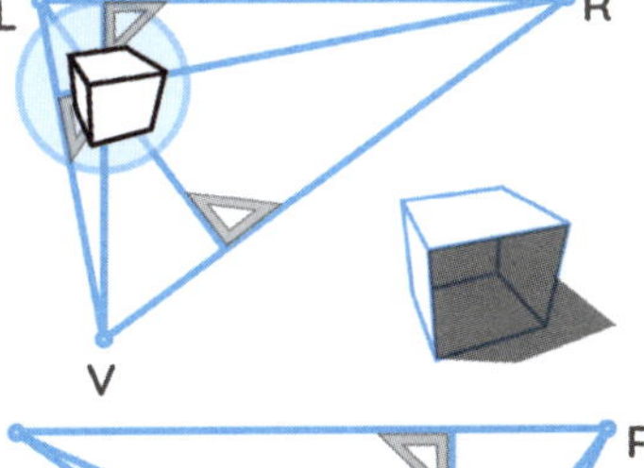

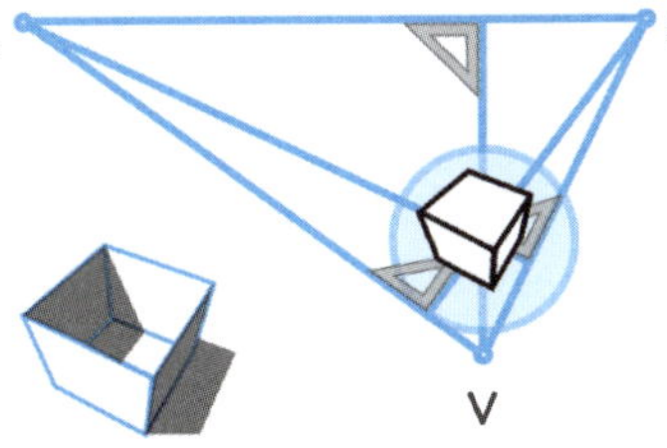

Panoramas

Deconstructing the Visual Field

According to the classical principle of perspective, it is not possible to draw a space encompassing 180° because in order to avoid distortions, we can only reconstitute about 60° of the angle (fig. 1). However, it is possible to cover the 180° of our visual field if we juxtapose at least three drawings (fig. 2).

Opposite, the three drawings of this interior space.

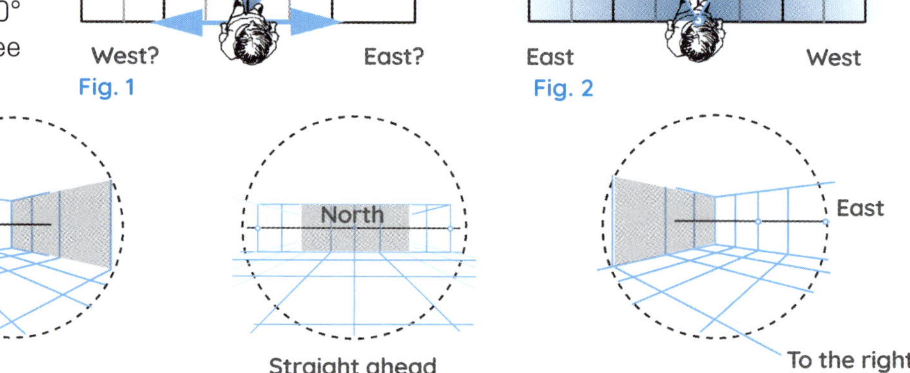

A 180° Overview

Juxtaposing the three drawings will allow us to make sense of the left and the right in our visual field. Thus, it becomes possible to gradually move from one point of view to the next by lightly curving the frontal lines that cross the drawing.

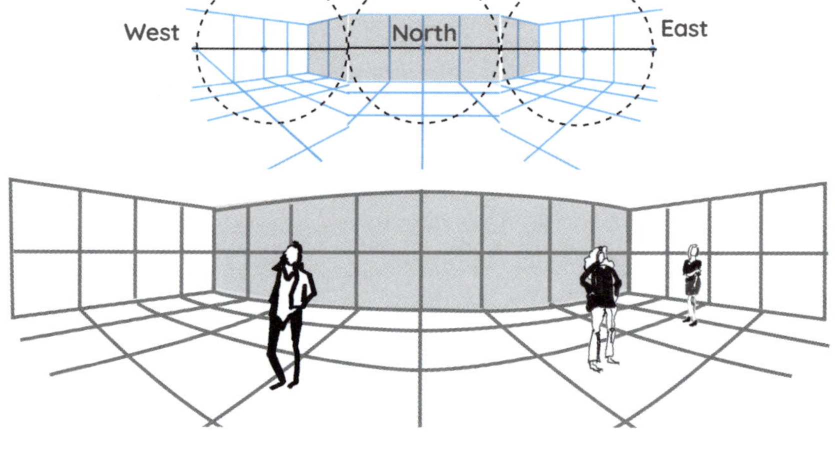

Interior, Marcillat-en-Combraille, central France

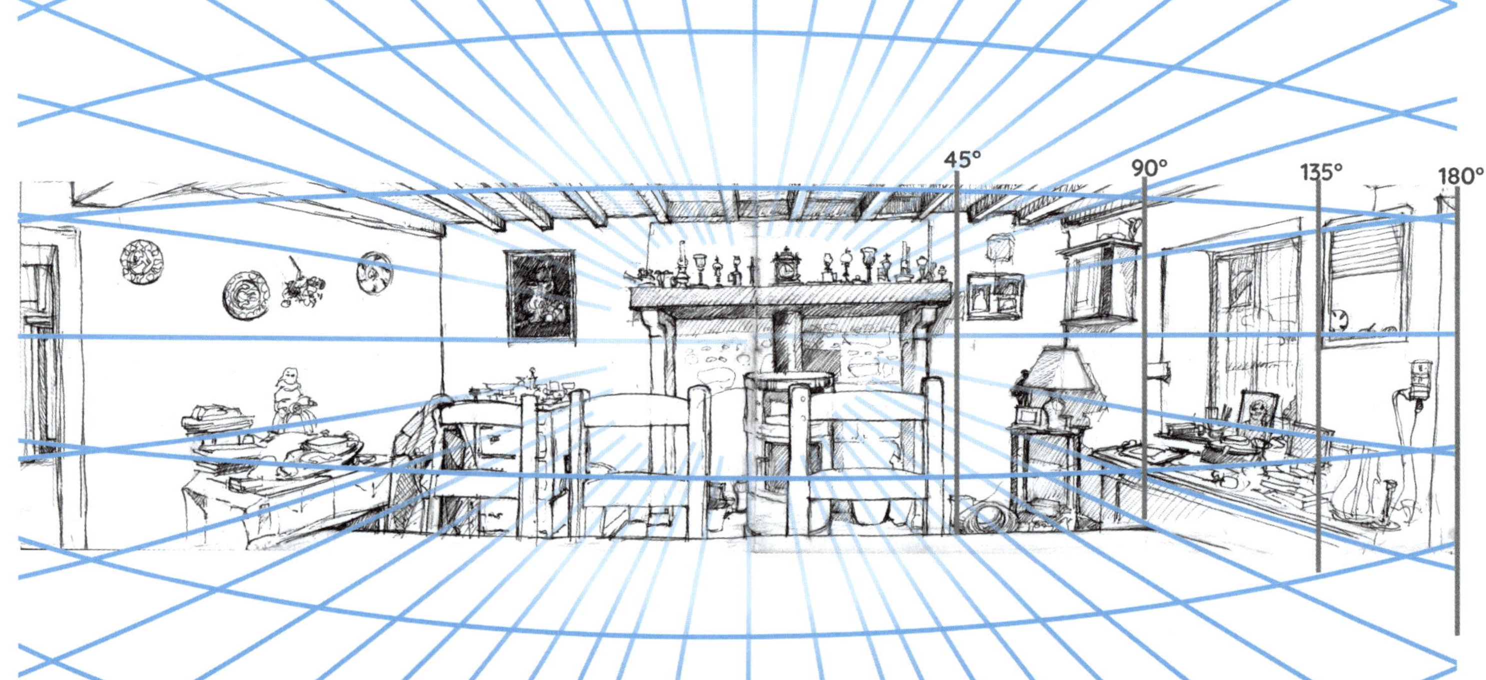

A Visual Walk

Panoramas invite us to take a walk with our eyes, because they involve a discreet juxtaposition of several points of view over a spread of 180°.

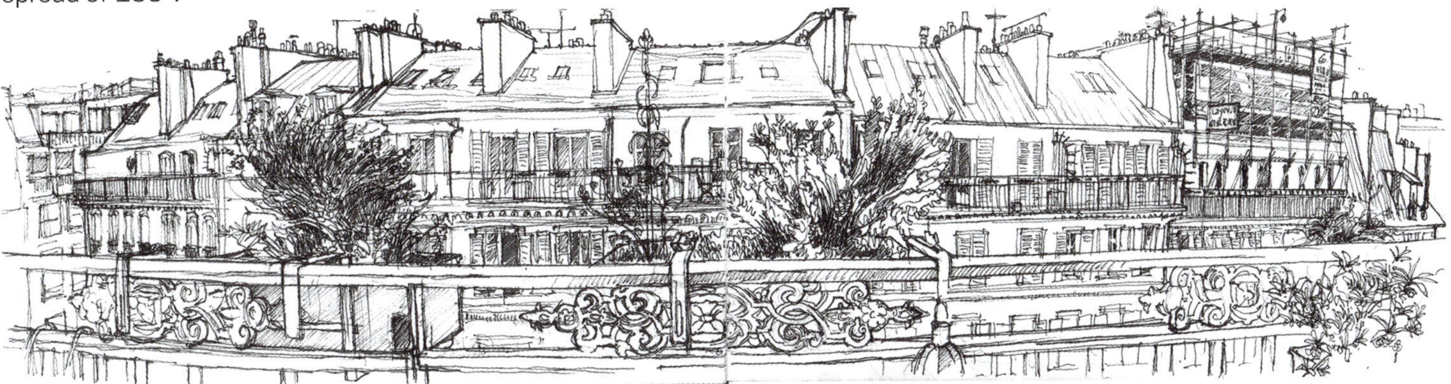

Paris, rue Paul Escudier

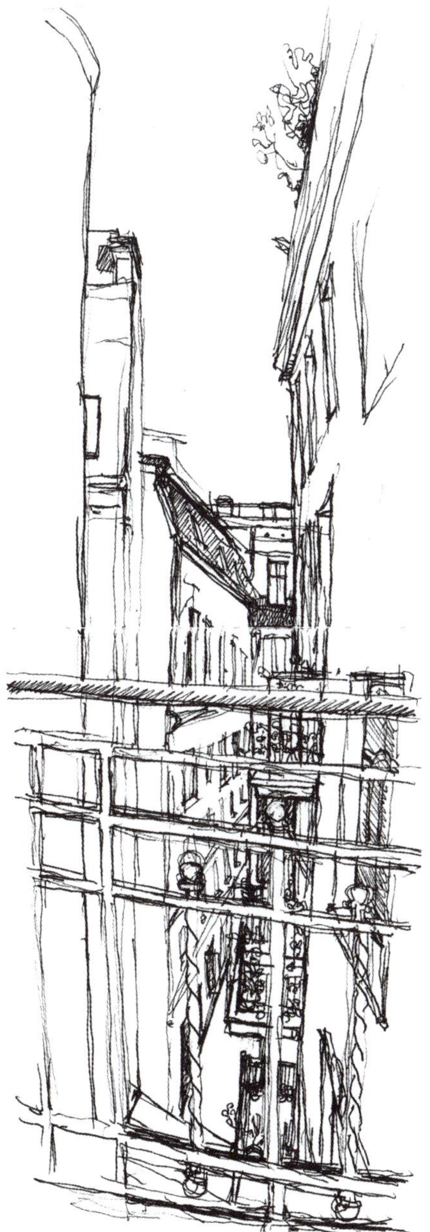

Vienna, Pension Riedl (Bed & Breakfast)

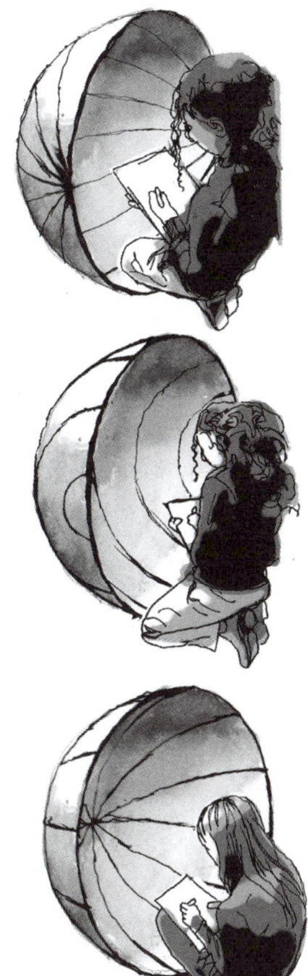

There are many different methods and solutions. The simplest thing is to keep to consistent juxtapositions and smooth transitions.

The curvature must remain subtle. It is not about forcing the viewer's gaze to the various parts of the drawing, but just about reaching the left and right sides as clearly and legibly as possible . . . in the same way that our brain does it. And our rationality trumps geometry.

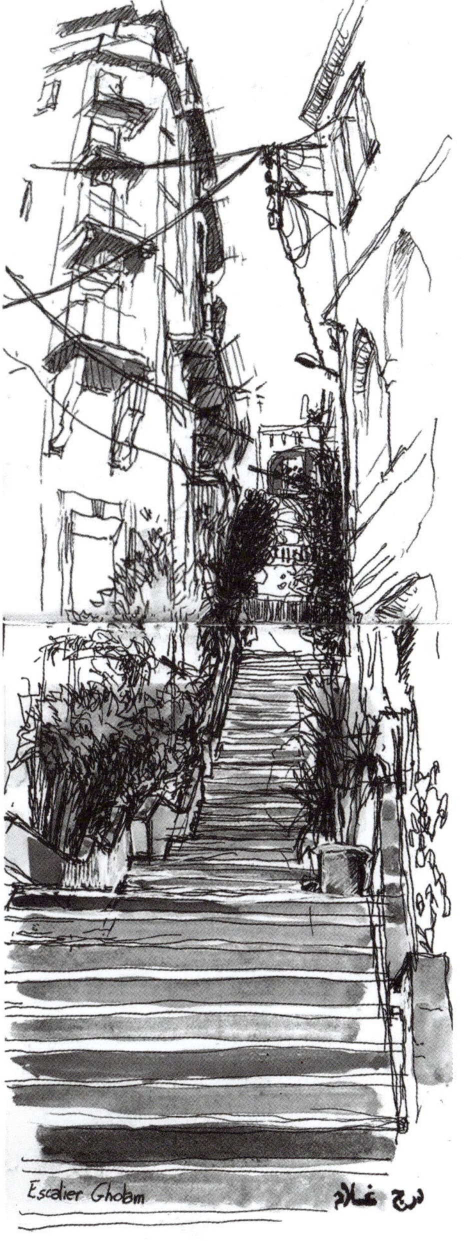

Beirut, Gholam Stairs

Panoramas

Resources

By the same author:

The Art of Perspective, Design Originals

Our Precursors:

For geometry: **Euclid** (3rd century BCE)

For optical geometry and physiology: **Ibn al-Haytham** (around 1000 CE)

Founder of projective geometry: **Girard Desargues** (17th century CE)

Pedagogy:

Ernest Norling, *Perspective Drawing*, Walter T. Foster

The Visual Approach:

Jason Cheeseman-Meyer, *Vanishing Point: Perspective for Comics from the Ground Up*, Impact Books

Neuroscience:

Alain Berthoz and Jean-Luc Petit, *The Physiology and Phenomenology of Action*, Oxford University Press

Alain Berthoz has published a number of other works with Éditions Odile Jacob that I also invite you to consult.

Perception:

Yves Le Grand, *Physiological Optics*, Springer

For French speakers (from the original French edition)

Geometric studies:

Louis Parrens, *Traité de perspective d'aspect: Tracé des ombres*, Éditions Eyrolles

Maurice Voilquin, *Géométrie descriptive*, "Durrande" collection, volumes 1 and 2

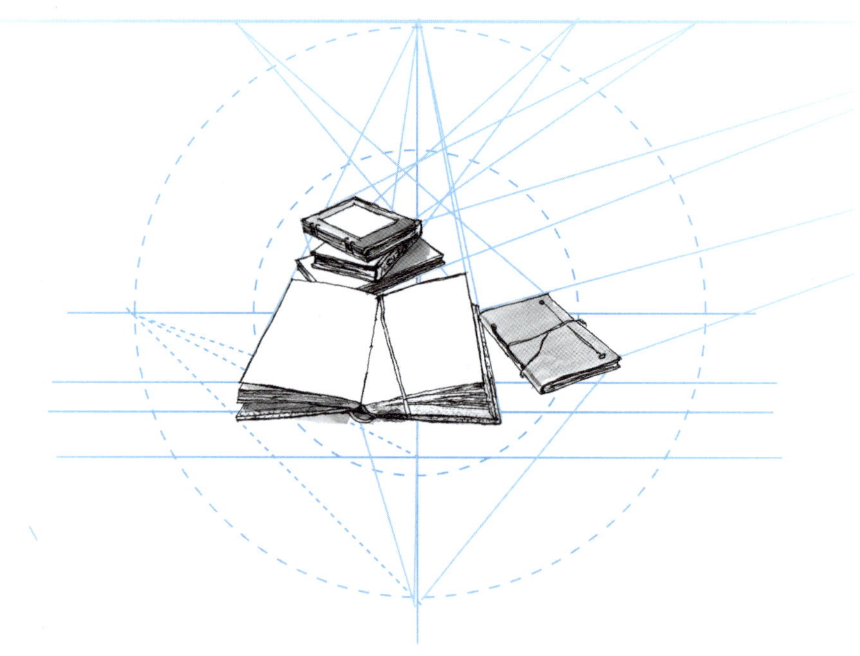